God Of The Untouchables

BY Dave Hunt

On the Brink
The Devil and Mr. Smith
Mission: Possible
God of the Untouchables

God Of The Untouchables

16064

Dave Hunt

Fleming H. Revell Company
Old Tappan, New Jersey

Scripture references in this volume are from the King James Version of the Bible.

Library of Congress Cataloging in Publication Data

Hunt, Dave.
    God of the untouchables.

    1. Gupta, Paul. 2. Converts from Hinduism.
3. Missions—India. I. Title.
BV269.G86H86   248′.246′0924 [B]   76–21858
ISBN 0–8007–0813–X

Contents

Foreword

The son of a high-caste Hindu moneylender, Vankateswami Gupta broke with tradition in a land steeped in religion. Upon his conversion he was renamed Paul after the great apostle, because of his unusual zeal.

Being convinced that Christ was the *only* way, he began to grow in his newfound faith as he introduced others to the life-changing God. Still in his teens he was put out of his home. Owning nothing more than the clothes on his back and a Bible, Paul learned to walk with God.

Miraculously, God fitted Paul with a helpmate, a conviction to begin a school that was true to the Bible, acceptance for schooling overseas, and funds for the trip to America.

I remember the day when Paul arrived in Los Angeles and began his seminary training. We all listened to his testimony of how the Lord led him to America. Before I graduated, my own life was enriched by his fervent zeal in the only True God he had come to know in India.

Dave Hunt has been able to capsulize the life of a modern George Mueller, who returned to his native land of India to multiply his life through the Hindustan Bible Institute graduates. I not only commend the book, but I urge Christians everywhere to read it and profit from it.

RUSSELL KILLMAN
Heaven and Home Hour
Glendale, California

1

The God That Demands Hair

"Hare Rama, hare Krishna . . . hare, hare. O Vankateswara, full of beauty, hear our prayers!"

The soft breeze stirring the cool night air blew the familiar chant like a giant whisper along the seemingly endless line of pilgrims climbing the steep slopes leading to the temple. All night they had worked their way up the steps cut into the mountainside, breathing heavily with the effort, pausing when need be to rest, then moving on with renewed determination toward their lofty goal. Some held kerosine lanterns high. Others stumbled forward in the darkness with scant help from the thin sliver of moon that hung precariously just above the horizon. The god Vankateswara, whose special abode was this famous temple at the top of the mountain, would smile upon them with favor for making this arduous climb. That hope gave strength to the weary.

Nagaruru Vankateswami Gupta stirred uneasily in his sedan chair and sleepily pushed back from his broad forehead the long strands of black hair that had never known scissors in the nine years since his birth. His mother was trudging doggedly beside him, remembering the vows she had made on this very mountain before the birth of her beloved Vankateswami, the apple of her eye, the son Vankateswara had given her. Never could that previous pilgrimage to Vankateswara's mountain lair be forgotten, which she and her husband had made as bride and groom right after their marriage. Kneeling fresh-shorn before the god, with every centimeter of their hair lying on the cold stones of the temple courtyard, they had made a solemn vow. If their prayer for a son was answered, they would dedicate him to Vankateswara.

The birth of a healthy, bawling boy a year later convinced them that their pilgrimage had brought its reward. As a seal to their pledge, they named the baby Vankateswami. (Nagaruru was the family name and Gupta the title of their Vaisya subcaste.) In gratitude they had vowed to return with their son as soon as he was old enough to worship at this holy shrine. The fulfillment of that pledge had brought them weary hours by bus and train and foot to join, on this happy night, the thousands stretched out in long column along the mountainside.

The east was red with coming dawn, and scores of pilgrims had already arrived ahead of them when Vankateswami's party of aunts, uncles, parents, grandparents, and assorted cousins, reached the summit and paused to rest in awesome view of the holy lake and the soaring, intricately carved towers of Vankateswara's temple just beyond. The jolt of his sedan chair hitting the ground awakened the boy bearing the god's name and he jumped out, rubbing his eyes.

"Are we here, Jaigee?" he called to the old woman crawling out of the chair that had been set down next to his.

Short and stout, and round of face, his father's mother was less stooped than one would expect for her age. Her long hair, rolled in its tight knot, was turning from gray to silver. Gingerly she stretched her cramped limbs, all the while smiling at her grandson, eyes twinkling with good humor and pride. Looking deeper into their dark depths one could see the glint of shrewdness that made her both feared and respected. Widowed now for some years, she was still the brains behind the scenes, guiding the business empire her dead husband had founded. Vankateswami's father, as the eldest of the six surviving sons, was the acknowledged head of the enterprises; but Jaigee's advice was always sought and followed.

Reaching over to tweak the small boy's cheek good-naturedly, she whispered seriously, "He who follows where the gods lead will reach his destination as surely as the paddy sprouts in its season." Except when she quoted well-known parts of the Vedas, few could discern whether her sayings were her own or something learned from her guru —but all respected her wisdom.

"Did the sun of my life sleep well?" His mother was standing behind him, running her fingers affectionately through the long, luxuriant locks that fell far below his shoulders. This beautiful hair would soon be lying with hers on the temple floor. Clenching her teeth, she drove from her mind the persistently whispered rumors that the hair given to the god found its way somehow to Hong Kong and Korea, where it was dyed blonde and reddish and other strange shades seldom seen in India, and made into wigs to be sold in America and Europe.

Stirring himself from where he had been leaning his tired back against a large rock, Vankateswami's father stood up wearily. "Come!" he said with a commanding tone and sweeping motion of his arm. "We've rested long enough. Look how many are getting ahead of us!" He moved toward the lake, bringing in his wake the many relatives who had gratefully accepted his generous offer to pay all expenses on this holy pilgrimage.

Leaving their sandals just outside with the busy attendants, the exuberant pilgrims filed through the high-arched gate. The cool stones of the temple courtyard felt deliciously refreshing to bare feet. Vankateswami followed in his father's footsteps, holding his hands over the sacred, purifying flame waved in front of him by the sweating, half-naked priest, then quickly putting hands against cheeks to feel the warmth; taking sacred ashes in fingers to make the familiar mark on forehead and neck, touching what remained to the tip of his tongue, murmuring the mantras after his father.

Waiting his turn, holding tightly to his mother's hand, Vankateswami watched the temple barbers work, expertly shaving heads with so few strokes, pausing only to sharpen their razors. The women seemed almost naked without hair. Caressing his own flowing locks, a wave of rebellion swept over him. Why should this god demand to have his hair? What did it do with it? Then he saw his mother's long, black, silken crown falling almost intact to the stones, felt the razor on his own head, and resentment turned suddenly to proud determination. To question the divine will was useless. Jaigee had already told him that many times, just as her guru had told her. The gods had their own reasons beyond the grasp of human understanding. One day he, too, would be a god, free at last from the illusions of fear and sorrow and tangible things.

Vankateswami's mother, looking so strange without hair that he hardly knew her, was holding his hand again, leading him across the courtyard, following his father. Impulsively he ran his fingers over his bare scalp. There was blood! Quickly he pulled his hand away, swallowing the impulsive cry that had started in his throat. He must be brave as his mother had taught him. In contrast to the shamefully averted gaze of the fresh-shaved low-caste women, his mother walked beside him with a proud upward tilt to her head and a look of fierce determination in her eyes that said it was an honor to give one's hair to this god who answers prayer.

He felt a tingling in his scalp. Already the sun god was healing the raw flesh. A good omen.

"The devils have been driven out of Vankateswami!" exclaimed the head priest of the Siva temple in Dugganapalli a few weeks after the pilgrims had returned. His listening subordinates nodded their heads gravely, without attempting, however, to hide the disbelief they still felt. Could shaving one's head really bring such a miracle? There were a number of other young rowdies in the village they would like to see make a pilgrimage to Tirupati!

"He is learning to see the true essence of life," continued the happy Brahmin. "Verily Vankateswara is a god that changes lives! Perhaps we should put up a shrine. . . ." A glance about the already crowded courtyard cut that suggestion short. The temple patron, Vankateswami's father, might be agreeable to funding an expansion—but that subject could only be broached at a propitious time. One dared not risk a negative response, for he was a man who stuck with his opinions when once expressed.

The priests in the Rama temple, built by Vankateswami's grandfather and still maintained by his father's largess, were no less astonished and certainly no less relieved by the remarkable change the pilgrimage to Tirupati had made upon this youngster who had been the terror of the temples. No longer did he run through the sanctuary at the head of a herd of rowdy youths, laughing and shouting insults to the gods.

Now all that was in the past. Praise be to Vankateswara! Miraculously a new boy had returned from Tirupati. Vankateswami's regular visits to both temples now brought warm smiles from the priests, and an occasional pat on the head and word of encouragement. The local pundit even predicted he would one day become a famous sadhu. The boy was a serious and earnest worshiper at the Siva and Rama temples and seemed truly devoted to all of the gods.

To the delight of his parents and Jaigee, the years that followed showed no lessening of Vankateswami's new religious zeal. Patient and tolerant of his younger brother, and unfailingly obedient to his parents, he was their joy and delight. By his early teens Vankateswami was paying exceptional attention to his personal dharma, and devoting himself to the path of action to improve his karma for the next life. The tastiest goat curry could not tempt him to break the Vaisya vow of vegetarianism; and so devoted was he to the doctrine of ahimsa that he would not wear leather goods of any kind without a guarantee that the animal had died of old age. His parents' pride in their firstborn was only exceeded by their love for him.

Sometimes Vankateswami felt he must be the luckiest boy in the whole world to have been born into such a happy family—but Jaigee scolded him for such modesty. "It's your karma," she insisted, "accumulated from good deeds in your past life."

"As the eldest son, some day you will take over the business," Vankateswami's father reminded him very seriously one hot and rainy afternoon as they sat together on the wide front porch, where the business was conducted, talking sporadically during a lull between the comings and goings of customers. "I want you to have more schooling than I got. Education is far more important now than it used to be, and Jaigee says it will become even more necessary."

Vankateswami's face brightened. "Then I shall go to high school in Proddutar?" he asked eagerly. "And live with Jaigee's brother and his family?"

His father nodded. "Yes. I have talked it over with Jaigee and your uncles, and we all agree. You are a bright boy, with a quick mind, and conscientious. You will do well in high school." He leaned forward, looking intently into his son's face. "After that we want you to go on to university to become a lawyer! You know what great advantage it would be with all the suits we have in court every year!"

Jumping to his feet, Vankateswami stood before his father as straight as a Bengali warrior at attention. "I shall not fail you, sir!" he said earnestly, his face flushed with emotion. "I will be the best lawyer the Guptas have ever had! You can count on that!"

The tortured memory of that lofty promise had haunted him during his second year at high school. He had meant it with all of his heart, and had never stopped wanting it to be true. That was what added confusion to the shame that overwhelmed him. In spite of his strongest resolve he had disgraced his family. Something beyond his power —evil forces, Jaigee called whatever it was—had invaded his mind and soul and driven him to a life of dissipation. And at such a young age! There was no controlling the mad compulsions that swept over him. All of his prayers to Vankateswara—and to Krishna, Rama, Siva, and every god he could think of—brought not the slightest change in his prodigal behavior. Indeed, the more he prayed the deeper he seemed to sink into sin and despair. Dharma had lost its meaning, the Vedas seemed irrelevant, and he knew that his karma was a disaster . . . but that affected the next life, and he now cared for nothing but the pleasure he could extract from the present moment.

The first year had gone well, with excellent grades. Then the money his father lavished upon him whenever he asked had made it possible not only to buy books and clothes, but to learn quite by accident how pleasurable it was to feast and drink at cafes until early morning. That had led to an association with bad companions who frequented such places. They drank and smoked heavily, gambled and caroused all over town; and before he knew it, Vankateswami not only had joined in but had become the ringleader. His parents didn't know what was happening, because his great uncle accepted without question his lies about studying late with friends.

Too late he realized that he had been lying to himself too, vowing again and again that "tonight is the last time; tomorrow I'll begin to study like a scholar!" Tomorrow never came. Finally he justified himself with the thought that no amount of studying would help: it was impossible to catch up, so he might just as well enjoy himself. His vow had changed to "Next year I'll do better." But next year didn't come either.

During the summer vacation he had mentioned casually that he would be taking several of his courses over again. Turning red with sudden anger, his father had demanded a full explanation. Dissatisfied with his son's lame excuses and suspecting now that he was lying, he went to Proddutar to learn the truth. What he discovered turned his anger into wild fury. There was no point in leaving the boy in school any longer.

And so at the age of seventeen Vankateswami found himself doing the tedious bookkeeping for the family business instead of studying to be a lawyer.

"See that you keep accurate accounts . . . and don't touch a rupee!" his father had growled through clenched teeth, like a judge sentencing a criminal.

Sitting cross-legged with the books of account on his lap, Vankateswami had looked at the floor, avoiding the angry eyes. It was true he had failed—but did his father really think he would steal? Never! He had learned his lesson. Everything would be different here away from his old companions. "A lamp in a place sheltered from the wind does not flicker," Jaigee had said without reproaching him. Expounding the virtues of a religious life, she had inspired him to renew his earlier vows.

How he regretted the swaggering and boasting about the court cases he was going to win for his father! It was easy to imagine what people were whispering behind his back; but there was nothing to do except hope that eventually the past would be forgotten.

What he hoped others would forget, however, continued to haunt him. The dream of becoming a lawyer meant too much and had been cherished too long to be relinquished without pain. That fond ambition, now turned to ashes but not forgotten, was like gravel in his throat, choking him with bitterness. What a poor bargain he had made, exchanging a bright future for a few months of sensual folly! His own stupidity puzzled him all the more because he had so fervently intended a much different kind of life.

"There is only one reality, one true Essence, and that is Brahman: all else is maya. You are God . . . you just don't know it yet. Look within and realize that you and Brahman are one, and you will be delivered from the illusion of fleshly passions." Jaigee had taught him this sacred truth before he could understand the words; and now that the words were in his vocabulary, he still couldn't understand. Truly the gods must know how hard he had tried, yet failed. If he was really of the same Essence as Brahman, and thus *was* Brahman, why then was it so difficult to realize what was true? Why did that which was only illusion seem always so real, so appealing—and the truth, the only Reality, seem so unreal and elusive?

Although his dream of becoming a lawyer would not be fulfilled, he must accept this as his karma. He could still become a good accountant. His father would yet be proud of him: but he must work hard, and honestly, and in time he would earn again the confidence that had been lost.

The business, after all, was interesting. Vankateswami enjoyed listening while his father or an uncle, sitting cross-legged on a mat, would converse with a customer facing them in the same posture.

They were moneylenders, and farmers came from a radius of thirty miles to borrow for a variety of reasons: to buy seed, or to get through a bad season when there had been no rain, or too much of it; or to pay rent when a crop had not come up to expectations. Frequent foreclosure of mortgages had made the Gupta brothers large land-holders—which necessitated keeping numerous servants in the fields, plowing, planting, weeding, harvesting. Selling the land and houses they acquired by default was just another business to be diligently pursued for profit. One was not in business to perform good deeds—that was a matter of religion, and the two never met.

As soon as the crops were harvested, many farmers were desperate to sell everything for whatever price they could get. Whether it was rice, corn, cotton, or whatever, the Guptas were ready to buy—at the right price, of course—and carefully sealed everything beneath the house in large storage rooms that extended out under the street. Thick walls of stone and cement not only kept out moisture and thieves, but frustrated even the huge rats that were known to gnaw and claw their way through the sides of buildings. With enough capital to buy in large quantities and the patience to wait, Vankateswami's father was always able to sell at higher prices later. This was not taking advantage of others—it was simply obedience to the law of supply and demand.

No loans were given without ample security, but often the farmer was only a tenant and owned no land. Reaching into his shirt to pull out a bag secured around his neck, from that he would draw out one at a time, reluctantly, gold earrings and necklaces and perhaps even a diamond or ruby, polishing each sadly as he laid it on the mat in front of him. The head of the Gupta enterprises would carefully and expertly examine each, the scrutiny punctuated by grunts and scowls and half-audible remarks about poor workmanship, poorer quality, and doubtful loan value. Gold objects would be mercilessly rubbed against the testing stone to see what mark they left in comparison to gold of known quality. Then followed the usual haggling, often heated and insulting. Though the opponents facing one another on the mat

varied, the feints, jabs, parries, and ploys were always the same
. . . and invariably the Gupta brothers won. It didn't take Vankateswami long to learn that money was power.

Although his father was very generous about buying clothes or
whatever else he needed, he refused to let him have any money to
spend. "It was the money I sent you at school that caused your
downfall," his father explained when Vankateswami complained. "I
won't make that mistake again. No money until I'm sure you're
cured!" That was the end of the matter. When his father had decided
something, there was no hope to change his mind by argument or
reason. Only time could do that, lots of time: but Vankateswami
couldn't wait. The more he brooded over the injustice of not having
even a rupee to call his own, the more overpowering the desire became
to take for himself some of the money that he counted at the end of
each day. Fear alone held him back. If he were discovered, that would
be a humiliation too great to bear! Then one day, almost like a gift
from the gods, came an unexpected opportunity.

"You must bring help! Quick!" An excited and panting farmer from
a nearby village had burst into their place of business, his face red
from heat and exhaustion.

The head of the Gupta empire seemed too surprised to move.
Vankateswami, the only other person there that day, sat transfixed
also.

"Don't just sit there!" the breathless farmer shouted. "Get help!"

"For what . . . and where?" Vankateswami's father yelled back,
finding his voice.

"Your brother, Bawala! They have him tied to a post and are
beating him mercilessly!"

The elder Gupta jumped to his feet. "Where is he?" he asked in a
voice that shook. His hands were trembling.

"It's Mohan Reddy and his sons. Bawala tried to collect a debt from
them. They overpowered him!"

Vankateswami's father was already going out the door. "Come on!"
he called, motioning to his son. "We'll get the constable in Proddutar

on our way! May the gods bring us there in time!"

Pushing the two bullocks as fast as they could pull the cart, they had gone less than half the distance to Proddutar when another cart approached. Hunched beside the driver was Bawala, so badly beaten that they hardly recognized him. He was a husky man with a hot temper, known as a vicious fighter, and apparently hadn't gone down easily.

"You're all right?" Vankateswami called anxiously.

"Do I look it!" he retorted, climbing down stiffly from the other cart. Paying the driver, he pulled himself up beside them. As the bullocks lumbered back toward home, he recounted the events of that memorable afternoon, speaking with great difficulty through swollen lips.

"The 10,000 rupees they owe us had been overdue for two months. I haven't been able to find them . . . until today." He wiped at a small trickle of blood oozing from his nose. "The devils! I gave them three days more, or we would take them to court and have their land. That was when all five of them jumped me. They didn't get off free. I put up a good fight!"

"How did you get away?" his elder brother interrupted.

"I didn't. They let me go. At first they threatened to kill me, and I thought they would do it. Two of them had big knives and murder in their eyes. They talked about where to hide the body. Then the old man had an idea. They offered me my freedom if I would sign a promissory note for 20,000 rupees."

"You didn't!"

"Of course I did. And so would you."

Vankateswami, sitting behind the two men, nodded his agreement.

"I would have signed a note for a million rupees to get away. It's worthless paper. Let them try to collect!"

"We won't wait for that! I'll see them in jail before dark!"

The excitement, with constables coming and going, lasted for days. Vankateswami's father was busy making reports, and the house was full of relatives from far and near expressing their sympathy to

Bawala, who seemed to enjoy the notoriety. There was whispered speculation out of Bawala's hearing whether he might not have participated in giving just such a beating to a helpless victim in his last life, and karma was catching up with him. Vankateswami trembled when he thought of what karma would do to him in the next life.

In all of the confusion it had been easy to take twenty rupees from the safe that first afternoon after his father had gone for the constable. He regretted not taking more. No one checked the books that day, nor the next, nor the next. All attention was on Bawala and the coming court case against the culprits, who had been quickly apprehended.

Vankateswami kept reminding himself that he had only taken a very little of what would one day be his. And it was for a worthy cause. There was a new movie he had to see in Proddutar. Driving there on the bullock cart a few nights later, he promised himself that he would avoid his old friends and come home directly after the show. The film was supposed to be a good one—about a monk who everyone thought was a reincarnation of Krishna, but who turned out to be the incarnation of a demon. A story like that was too important to miss.

2

In Search of Salvation

"Sneak thief! Robbing your own family!"

"I'm sorry . . . I didn't mean to do it!"

"Like I don't mean *this!*" His father gave him another hard slap across the face.

"He didn't mean to doctor the books either. His pen just did it by itself," growled his uncle Terukalaya sarcastically. The plants from which indigo was extracted grew profusely in the fields around Proddutar, and Terukalaya sold the hardened cakes of concentrated dye to cloth merchants in the Bombay area. Returning from a trip, he had been looking through the business records and happened to discover the latest embezzlement.

When the first twenty rupees he had taken had gone undiscovered, Vankateswami had been encouraged to do the same thing again . . . and again. Soon it had become a way of life. His father had eventually caught him and slapped him around the porch with the help of his uncles until his face had burned with the stinging blows. But the smarting pain of shame within had been far worse than the throb of his swollen cheeks. He had promised never to do it again, and had meant it: but his highest resolve was no match for the morbid craving to have his own money that dominated his life. Weary of this continual inner struggle, he would give in on the condition that this would be "the last time." Of course it never was.

Far worse, however, than the shame and guilt and inner turmoil was the fear that the horrible prediction his father made each time he caught him would indeed come true: "If you keep this up, you're going straight to hell! Do you hear me? Straight to *hell!*"

Vankateswami would stand with drooping shoulders, head bent forward, eyes to the floor, trembling inside. It wouldn't be long, however, until everyone would be jovial again as though all was forgiven and forgotten. His father would pat him on the back and tell him to cheer up . . . but Vankateswami couldn't get the thought of hell, nor the fear of it, out of his mind. Once he had been confident that karma would make him something better in the next life, perhaps even a Brahmin. Now he feared that his evolution could only be downward, to become a rat, or hated scorpion, pushed ever lower by his karma . . . to drop at last into the flames of hell with no escape. Hadn't Jaigee herself said that transmigration of the soul could be downward as well as upward?

The family had recently made a pilgrimage to Benares on the banks of the Ganges where the elderly waited to die, hopeful that if their dead bodies were committed to its sacred waters they would go directly to heaven. He had bathed in that Mother of all rivers, but felt no sense of purification from sin. The old fear of hell still haunted him, yet he hadn't stopped stealing. Indeed he couldn't. Should he return there to drown himself in the Ganges? Would that assure him of nirvana? If he could only be certain . . . but there were so many divergent opinions from hundreds of gurus all claiming to be the present living reincarnation of Rama, Krishna, and Christ. There was, however, another way to escape hell that almost all agreed upon. Some of his cousins had paid large sums to the priests for special pujas to get their cremated parents into nirvana. But what if there wasn't enough money . . . or suppose his heirs weren't willing to pay the price?

"How are you seeking salvation?" he asked Jaigee very earnestly one evening in private. Less interested in the business and more concerned with preparing for the next life, she was growing daily more feeble, but her mind was still sharp.

"There are many paths," she replied thoughtfully. "Yoga is the

best, but few are able to practice such strict discipline. Each must seek
his own dharma. If one does more good than evil, at least the progres-
sion is upward from one life to the next. . . ."

"And if one's evil deeds outweigh the good . . . ?" he interrupted.

She looked at him sympathetically. "Speak and worship the sacred
syllable *Om.* This is the Supreme Brahman. It is said that *'Om* is the
bow, one's Self is the arrow, Brahman is the target.' By repetition of
Om and meditation you will find your true Self."

"I repeat it more times than I can count—and all the best mantras
—but still I have no peace. I am afraid of hell!"

"Manu has said, 'Nonviolence, truthfulness, nonstealing, purity,
sense control—this is the dharma of all four castes.' Follow this rule."

"I have tried without success." Suddenly he felt angry. Others had
failed too. "No one fully follows the Vedas!" he grumbled. "Not even
the Brahmins. It is no secret about the girls who stay so long in the
temples. In our own village I have heard. . . ."

"It's certain that stealing is wrong!" she interrupted sharply, cut-
ting off any further accusations against the priesthood, though she
knew there was justification. "It is unbecoming for a thief to accuse
others!"

"I take nothing that isn't my own, what my father refuses to give
me. Just wages. He is unreasonable."

"It is stealing," she said firmly, but the sharpness had left her voice.
He was her favorite in spite of recent events.

"Sometimes it is right to steal," he argued defensively. "Even the
gods have stolen. It is said that Krishna steals the women's saris when
they bathe."

"It isn't the same!" she said indignantly. Her voice softened again.
"You will change. I have much faith in you."

This was not the subject he had intended to talk about and it made
him uncomfortable. "You didn't answer my question," he reminded
her. "How do *you* seek salvation?"

"I have hope that my karma will bring me to nirvana within five
more reincarnations. So my guru tells me . . . but nothing is certain

except writing the sacred name of Rama. I have filled books with his name. Perhaps some day you could count them for me."

"Of course. How many times do you wish to write it?"

"It is said that anyone who writes *Rama* 100 million times will reach nirvana without fail."

"That is a lot of writing," said Vankateswami thoughtfully. "Far easier to die beside the Ganges so one's body could be given to the sacred waters."

"I have written it five thousand times in a single day, but my fingers grow ever more stiff with age. I do not count very high, but others say I have already written five million. If you would do a favor for an old woman, tell me the true count."

Always quick with figures, Vankateswami had been calculating rapidly in his mind: 5,000 a day was about 1,800,000 a year, which left more than fifty years to go. It would not be a kindness to an old woman to tell her that. "Someday I will count them for you," he said absently. "Someday."

"Jaigee! Jaigee! Where are you?"

Vankateswami's mother pushed her way through the curtain hanging across the open doorway and hurried to Jaigee, wringing her hands. "Your youngest brother . . . they don't think he'll live!" She burst out crying, unable to talk anymore.

"He's only fifty!" Jaigee wailed, on her feet now, looking puzzled and alarmed.

Vankateswami's father had entered the room and was standing just inside the door, beckoning for his mother. "I've called for the bullock cart," he said quietly. "Come. I'll go with you."

It was late that night before the two returned from Proddutar, exhausted and heartbroken, with a strange tale. Jaigee's youngest brother had been famous for his accomplishments in yoga, and was a well-known wrestler, excelling in a sport that the Moslems had too long dominated. Vankateswami had seen very little of this famous man who seemed always to be secluded in his room practicing yoga or away in the gymnasium where the local wrestlers gathered. But he remembered well what Jaigee had so often told him.

"He's a great yogi!" she had often said with ill-concealed pride. "Sitting in lotus position, by the power of his mind he can lift himself almost to the ceiling!"

"Have you seen him do it?" Vankateswami had asked in awed tone when he first had heard this as a small boy.

She had nodded gravely. "I . . . and very few others. It is a sacred practice, not for the eyes of the world."

Now he was dead. Apparently he had decided upon a public demonstration of his powers. With a crowd of people watching he had attempted a front flip from the top of the roof, but had landed on his face and never regained consciousness. Some thought he had reached nirvana. Others said it was a premature death, and therefore his spirit must wander, haunting family and friends. No one knew for sure.

Unfortunately the funeral came at a very busy time for the money-lenders. Business, of course, was always first, as Jaigee well knew; so she carried her six sons' apologies to Proddutar when she paid her last respects to her brother's ashes. Vankateswami was secretly glad he couldn't go. He had developed a strong aversion for funerals, with their long processions, drums beating, mourners wailing, Brahmin priests chanting mantras and waving the sacred flame. It left him unnerved for days, viewing a corpse—and how could one avoid that at a cremation ceremony, with the body laid out on the carefully stacked logs soaked in kerosine or dotted with camphor, to be ignited by the eldest son, the widow beating her breasts and wailing unconsolably just behind him. It always reminded him that one day his body, too, would lie lifeless on a pile of logs, leaping flames turning it to ashes . . . while his soul would doubtless be tormented in the depths of hell by even hotter flames.

"You're obsessed with hell," one of his uncles suggested. "There is no such place—so don't worry. Vedanta teaches that this life is but a dream from which we will awaken to oneness with the Absolute. Life, death, heaven, hell, good, evil—none of them really exist. So don't take this dream so seriously."

"Then why do you scold me for stealing?"

"One has to be practical also," he said irritably, and broke off the conversation.

Vankateswami had already tried to adopt the view that all was maya, but without success. It didn't help to tell himself that his thievery was just an illusion—the torment of guilt and fear of hell were still there. Regularly at the temples, perambulating around the shrines in the courtyards, giving money to the priests—money he had stolen from his father—Vankateswami found no peace. The gods seemed unable, or unwilling, to help him. When the wind caught a sari, making it cling to a girl, outlining her hips or thighs or breasts, he would hate himself for the thoughts that filled his mind. Hands stretched out to the warmth of the sacred flame extended by the priest, then fingers pressed firmly against his forehead, he would pray fervently to the gods, without success, for strength to overcome the evil that raged within him . . . and for salvation from hell. It was the latter that concerned him the most.

Then one day while Jaigee's guru was visiting her, Vankateswami decided to seek his advice. When he heard the familiar sounds of farewell, he entered the room where they had been talking and prostrated himself before the Master, a man about sixty years of age. The guru's long gray hair was matted with dirt, and his full white beard, framing a rather pleasant wrinkled face, covered most of the black beads hanging down the front of his saffron robe.

"I know your desire," he said, motioning to Vankateswami to arise. "Your grandmother says you fear hell and seek salvation."

"Yes, Master. I have tried the path of action, but my bad deeds grow faster than the good. Truly I need your help!"

"You are too young to have such heavy concerns," the guru replied soothingly. "Is there not much happiness in youth?"

"I do not wish to be happy now only to land in hell!"

"In the Vedanta it is said, 'For him who knows the true Self both good and evil are alike; indeed, both do please the Self for him who knows thus. This is the secret teaching.' "

"I do not understand."

"You concern yourself too much with good and evil and karma, and have neglected the way of knowledge."

"Yes!" exclaimed Vankateswami eagerly. "That is because I have no guru to teach me!"

Bowing toward Jaigee, her guru started for the door. Vankateswami jumped into his path. "Holy Master! I will be your follower, cook your food, wash your clothes . . . only lead me on the path of divine enlightenment!"

Palms together in front of him, smiling, the holy man half bowed again. "What do you know of the Scriptures?"

"I know many mantras and have read the Vedas, perhaps not as diligently as I should. . . ." Vankateswami hung his head.

"The Bhagavad-Gita is the Book of books. Read it faithfully every day for six months . . . and then I will examine you. If you are worthy, I will be your guru."

That promise was like a benediction and gave Vankateswami new hope. The family's only copy of the Bhagavad-Gita was in Sanskrit. Determined to learn all he could, he read it aloud each morning when the business opened, and his father and uncles would correct his pronunciation and explain the deeper meanings. Six months would pass quickly, and then he would be a follower of this great guru, and his salvation would be assured. It troubled him somewhat that Jaigee, who had been taught by this guru for years, seemed so uncertain of her own salvation. But his case was different: He was younger, and could do what she could not. There was hope, for the first time in months.

He was familiar in a general way with the Bhagavad-Gita, but reading it daily brought new appreciation. Indeed it was the Book of books. He fell in love with it. The narrative style made the truth much easier to grasp. Krishna would forever be his favorite among the gods.

Then one morning, with several customers standing about listening as he read, in one terse sentence in chapter 4 his beloved Bhagavad-

Gita snuffed out that last ray of hope he had been nurturing, leaving him in darkness and utter desolation:

> **Lord Krishna came to save the righteous and**
> **to condemn the sinners.**

Reading the words again, Vankateswami asked each of his listeners who knew the Sanskrit well to explain the meaning. When all had agreed with what he himself had easily understood, he closed the Book of books in despair. His doom was sealed. Lord Krishna was the kindest, the closest to man of all the gods, the reincarnation of Vishnu the Preserver, who came to show men the way of salvation . . . but he had come to save only the righteous and to condemn the sinners! No salvation for sinners? Then there was no salvation for him!

Walking slowly into the house, he put the Bhagavad-Gita in its place on the shelf beside the family gods. Then he went back to the books of account, but the figures on the page were blurred and meaningless. Something inside him had died.

3

Power in the Blood

The drums had been beating for over an hour. Looking up from his work, Vankateswami had a perfect view of the goddess Moolamma's temple facing his house from the other side of the small square. With growing excitement he had watched the farmers and their families—running, laughing children, wives and young women in dazzling, multihued saris—arriving in a steady stream through the port gate to his right, gathering in front of the temple, which was far too small to accommodate the large crowd on this annual festival day. In his younger years the executioner's slashing sword and spurting blood used to frighten him—but this had become Vankateswami's favorite religious festival. Certainly it was the most exciting. Perhaps its very gruesomeness and violence made it peculiarly appealing in a society where the devout wouldn't kill an ant or a fly and everyone was dedicated to nonviolence, inspired not only by the ancient writings, but of late by the courageous example of Mahatma Gandhi, who was slowly breaking Britain's grip on India by passive resistance.

There was nothing passive in this ritual. At last! There it was, the day's sacrifice, being pulled and pushed by three men through the crowd until they were in front of the image of the goddess, where they held it—a large buffalo, the gray mud scrubbed from its back until it was shining and clean.

Of course the law of ahimsa was supposed to be followed at all times by all Hindus; but as Vankateswami had already learned, there were exceptions to every rule. What devout Hindu did not revere Kali,

consort of Siva, at whose temple in Calcutta animals were sacrificed
by the hundreds, ahimsa notwithstanding? Was not Kali's beauty in
her bloodthirstiness? Often pictured with freshly severed human
heads and hands hanging as garlands about her, a goblet of warm
human blood in her hands, she lived by killing her sons and daughters
among men. Who could therefore doubt that a blood sacrifice was
what, above all, she wanted? Ramakrishna himself had been one of
her most adoring devotees, and who was a greater Hindu or a truer
one than he?

Though not as famous as Kali, Moolamma, too, required fresh
blood. Often goats would be slain for her by plunging their necks
down onto the sharp stake that stood upright in front of her temple.
Once every year, however, when the paddy was planted a buffalo had
to be offered, and prescribed ritual followed in order to assure the
blessing of Moolamma, goddess of fertility, upon the surrounding
fields for another season.

Absorbed in the excitement and intricate ritual unfolding before
him now, Vankateswami forgot momentarily the despair that had
gripped him since reading in the Bhagavad-Gita that there was no
salvation for sinners. Although he had watched this every year since
childhood, today again the whirling, frenzied dancers fascinated him
as always, and the drums and horns made his foot tap with the steady
rhythm. The beat quickened, and every eye was riveted upon the
stalwart young sword-wielding farmer who had joined the priest in
front of the goddess and the victim. This year's executioner, as always,
had been chosen for his unusual strength, for the thick neck of the
pawing buffalo must be severed with one blow.

The highly polished, glittering sword, sparkling like a diamond in
the sun, suddenly flashed in lightning-swift arc. A heavy shudder went
through the buffalo's body, and then without a sound its knees buck-
led and the stricken creature rolled over onto the ground, quivering,
the severed head coming to rest a few feet away. Quickly the sacred
vessels were placed to catch the precious blood draining from the
neck. The chanted mantras and blessings of the priest accompanied

by the murmured responses of the worshippers were punctuated by the now slowed and softened beating of the drums as uncooked rice was stirred into the warm blood. Farmers pressed forward eagerly to take their share as one by one they left to spread this red-stained offering on their fields. There was power in that blood. Power to bring forth healthy plants from the ground and to assure a good harvest, the special blessing of goddess Moolamma . . . unless the monsoon god, or the god of drought, or the god of blight interfered with a stronger power.

Several days later a white man he had never seen, accompanied by several Untouchables, invaded the Vaisya community through the port gate and stood in the square in a small group facing Vankateswami's house, their backs to Moolamma's now deserted temple. While one of the Indians played a harmonium and two others kept time with a tambourine and a tiny drum, the group sang loudly several incomprehensible songs about a strange god called Jesus. Their drab performance seemed a pitiful contrast to the exciting and colorful ritual that had been acted out on this square so recently. The tall white man was obviously a missionary. Vankateswami had heard of such people, but had never come into contact with one before.

Vankateswami knew nothing about Christ, only that there was a community of the followers of this strange god outside nearly every village he had ever seen. Even his own village had a small community of Christians, removed by half a mile from the main settlement because they were Untouchables. It was the Law of Manu to isolate such people, who were despised by the gods themselves. That was reason enough for every caste Hindu to reject Christ; but worse yet, Christians called the Hindu gods myths, and ate the meat of the cow, the sacred Mother of us all!

Vankateswami had been absorbed in trying to cover in the books his most recent theft. The loud singing distracted his thoughts and made it difficult to add the figures. Dropping his pen with a grunt of disgust, he straightened up and began wearily rubbing his tired back.

The words ringing across the square were offensive to anyone who adhered to ahimsa, as every Hindu must:

> **Would you be free from your burden of sin?**
> **There's power in the blood . . .**
> **. . . the precious blood of the Lamb!**

Not only was the song offensive, but it made no sense. A lamb was much smaller than a buffalo. Obviously white men knew nothing about the goddess Moolamma. Trying again to concentrate upon his work, he was distracted by another song:

> **O the blood of Jesus, the precious blood of Jesus!**
> **O the blood of Jesus, that cleanses from all sin!**

Blood that cleanses from all sin? He could understand the logic of bloodstained rice bringing fertility to the land it was sprinkled upon, for the rice itself was of the soil. But how could the blood of a lamb cleanse from sin? And this Jesus . . . was he after all a lamb and not a god? It hardly mattered—the god of the Untouchables was no god for him. And with millions of gods, why should any Hindu want another?

The singing stopped. Vankateswami picked up his pen again and tried to concentrate on his work. The missionary's loud, booming voice made that impossible. He was waving a black book in his hand and shouting to the whole world that it was the revelation of the true and only God, the Creator, telling the way of salvation. Opening it, he began to read:

> **This is a faithful saying, and worthy of all**
> **acceptation, that Christ Jesus came into the**
> **world to save sinners . . . (I Timothy 1:15).**

To save *sinners!* Vankateswami was hanging onto every word, his work forgotten. Could there really be salvation for *sinners?* For *him?* A small crowd had gathered, perhaps thirty or forty Sudras and Vaisyas. Even a Brahmin was hovering near the edge of the square, trying to look as though he wasn't listening. The stranger with the pale skin was explaining that this Jesus was the very God that created the entire universe; yet he had come to this earth as a man to save sinners. There it was again—to save *sinners!* He had lived a perfect, sinless life, healing the sick, raising the dead, feeding the hungry, teaching men to love even their enemies—but he had been hated. Men had nailed his hands and feet to a cross, plunged a spear into his side, and there he had died as a sacrifice for our sins willingly, because he loved us. On the third day he had been resurrected—*not* reincarnated —and had gone back to heaven, but was coming again to this earth to set up his kingdom.

"There is power in the blood of Jesus to deliver from sin's penalty," the missionary explained. "Sin is rebellion against our Creator, taking our own way instead of living as he intended. God said, 'The wages of sin is death. . . .' [Romans 6:23.] We rebel again and try to escape this righteous penalty, clinging desperately to life, afraid to die. But Jesus was willing to die for us all. He said, 'Follow me to my cross, accept my death as your very own, die with me, and you will share in my Resurrection, for I will live in you.' [*See* Matthew 16:24, 25.] You need have no fear of hell. The penalty has been paid. Believe this good news and you will have the peace of those who have been forgiven."

For hours after the stranger left, his words were still ringing in Vankateswami's ears. It was too good, too simple, to be true. According to the Bhagavad-Gita, salvation was much more difficult than that. Krishna would not save the sinners, but they might save themselves, for he had said to Arjuna, "Even if thou art the most sinful of sinners thou wilt cross over all transgression by the raft of divine knowledge." But there was no clear explanation of how to attain this knowledge, and the gurus gave many interpretations. It was thought to come by yoga, for Krishna had said again, "There is no purifier on earth equal to divine knowledge. A man who becomes perfect in yoga finds it in himself in the course of time." Yet yogis who had practiced all their lives still sought oneness with Brahman. If Christ's offer seemed too simple, surely yoga was too difficult. Self-realization was attempted by many, but who had ever really achieved it? Certainly no one in his village, nor anyone he had ever heard of, not even the priests, nor Jaigee's younger brother. Would simply believing that Christ had died for his sins give that inner peace that he had sought unsuccessfully? It seemed preposterous. And yet, if God would forgive. . . .

Indeed, if there were forgiveness, then karma was obsolete, and the whole idea of reincarnation was meaningless. The cycle of rebirth into future lives was only a means by which karma could exact its due. But if God could forgive sinners because Christ had died for them, then karma had nothing to exact. His head throbbed.

Closing the books, Vankateswami walked outside, leaving his father and uncles absorbed in their conversations with customers. The smell of jasmine was thick in the air. He breathed deeply, and watched two blackbirds pursue a squawking crow out of sight. There was only one thing to do. He *must* read this book for himself. Clapping his hands, he called a servant and sent him to the Untouchables' village to borrow a New Testament.

At first he read secretly. Much he didn't comprehend, but it took no great understanding to see that the main message of the New Testament was salvation for sinners through Christ's death and Resurrection. The more he read, the louder his conscience seemed to say, "This is the salvation you have been seeking. Why don't you receive it? Krishna came to save the righteous, but what salvation did *they* need? Who will save sinners—like *you*—if not this Jesus?" He wrestled with that question for weeks.

Eventually he began reading the New Testament aloud each morning when the office opened for business, just as he had once read the Bhagavad-Gita. His father and uncles paid little attention and made no complaint. Customers would linger on and listen as long as he kept reading. Villagers, and even strangers, crossing the square and hearing his loud voice would come and stand in front of the house, seemingly drawn by the story of Jesus.

In contrast to the Bhagavad-Gita, which had seemed mystical, obscure, and at times contradictory, this Jesus spoke so simply and directly—and not of religion or philosophy, but of himself: "I have come to seek and to save the lost . . . I am the way, the truth and the life, no man comes to the Father but by me . . . I and my Father are one . . . before Abraham was, I am . . . search the Scriptures, for they testify of me . . . come unto me, all ye that labor and are heavy laden, and I will give you rest . . . if any man thirst, let him come unto me and drink . . . I am the good shepherd who gives his life for the sheep . . . I am the resurrection and the life . . . the hour is coming when all that are in the graves shall hear my voice and come forth . . . and then many will say to me, 'Lord, Lord, haven't we done miracles in your name?' And I will say to them, 'Depart from me, I never knew you.' . . . for not every one who merely calls me Lord will enter into the kingdom, but those who do my Father's will . . . and this is his will, that you believe on me."

Jesus was not preaching a path of knowledge, nor of difficult works, nor self-realization through yoga and endless repetition of the syllable *Om*. That was abundantly clear. His statements were staggering in their simplicity and frightening in their blunt directness: "Judge not, lest you be judged . . . he who hears my words and obeys them not is like a fool building a house without foundation on sand . . . the words that I have spoken will judge you in that day . . . I am the light of the world." All men stood condemned in his presence, yet he forgave those who repented and believed in him.

Everything Jesus said contradicted the religion Vankateswami had been taught, and that troubled him. The truth of truths for every Hindu was that he was God: but Jesus taught that *he alone* of all men was God, and every other man was separated from God by sin. The great objective of Hinduism was God-consciousness through divine knowledge: Jesus urged men to receive the benefits of God's love through faith in him. Yoga was a set of methods for looking within oneself to find God: Jesus taught that men must turn from themselves to him. Hinduism was a system of do-it-yourself salvation through prayer, ritual, pilgrimages: Jesus said that men must admit the impossibility of saving themselves and accept his sacrifice for their sins. Krishna had taught Arjuna that everything but Brahman is illusion, and assured him that it wasn't wrong to kill because one only kills the unreal body and not the Self, which cannot be killed. But Jesus taught men to love even their enemies, and to lay down their own lives, not to take the lives of others.

Weeks stretched into months and still he read the New Testament aloud each day, now thoroughly convinced that Christ and Krishna were not merely different manifestations of the same God. Hundreds of gurus in India claimed to be the latest reincarnation of the "Christ spirit." They couldn't all be right. Were any of them? Not according to this Book, which claimed that Christ's birth through a virgin in Bethlehem had brought him for the very first time to earth, not as an avatar, but as God becoming man only once to die for our sins, finishing the work of salvation once for all.

Jesus claimed to be the *only* way . . . and if that was true, then Krishna was wrong. They couldn't both be right. Vankateswami mulled over that for weeks, seeking desperately to escape the logic of it. Gandhi had admired Jesus while remaining a Hindu. Pondering that deeply, Vankateswami concluded that, as much as he respected Gandhi, it didn't make sense. If Jesus was just another god, then why bother with him at all? Hinduism already had more than enough gods. It was his uniqueness that made Jesus desirable. He alone had died for our sins, been resurrected, and promised forgiveness and eternal life to all who would believe in him. There was no other god like that! If Jesus was who he claimed to be, then all the rest were frauds.

That was the rub. It was bad enough to embrace the Untouchables' God. But if accepting Jesus' death for our sins was the *only* way, then the perfect practice of yoga, holy baths in the Ganges, offerings to the idols, the pursuit of mystic knowledge and god-consciousness through meditation could only be what Jesus called "climbing up another way, as a thief and a robber" (*see* John 10:1). It was like dying to accept this Jesus, dying to life as one would have lived it. No wonder Jesus had said that to be his disciple one must deny himself, take up the cross, and follow him. Vankateswami was afraid. To accept this Jesus would cost him everything.

Great crises are often resolved in unexpected and simple ways. He was reading aloud from the New Testament as usual, with several customers listening, and had reached the eighth chapter of Hebrews. The twelfth verse, like a number of others throughout this book, had been underlined by the owner in red ink. Vankateswami read it twice because it seemed so important. "For I will be merciful to their unrighteousness, and their sins and their iniquities will I remember no more." He let his eyes run over the words again, and something inside him said, "Yes, I'll believe that. God can forgive me because Jesus died for my sins."

"I will be merciful to their unrighteousness. . . ." He had struggled so long and so hard to become righteous, without success. How he needed God's mercy and forgiveness! He needed a salvation that didn't depend upon his own merits but upon the sacrifice of one who had been able to die in his place. ". . . their sins and their iniquities will I remember *no more.*" That promise took away his fear. It had been settled forever.

"Thank you, Lord," he said under his breath. "Thank you." The crisis had passed almost without his realizing it.

There was no longer any reason to march around an idol shrine, nor to offer coconuts to gods that couldn't eat them, nor to mark his forehead and neck with ashes and prostrate himself before images of wood and stone. He worshiped no more the family idols enshrined in their corner of the dining room, avoided the family puja, and went outside to talk with his heavenly Father when the pundit arrived on his weekly rounds to bless the business with special incantations for a fee. The fear of hell had vanished like the morning mist under a burning sun.

The New Testament became like food to his soul, but there was also much he didn't understand as he read. Like the verse he noticed in Mark 16 one day: "He that believeth and is baptized shall be saved; but he that believeth not shall be damned" (verse 16). The word "baptized" had been left untranslated because there was no Telugu equivalent. How could he find out what it meant? Whatever it was, he must do it.

Inexpressible emotions surged and tumbled around in Vankateswami late that afternoon as he made his way resolutely through the Untouchables' village toward the chapel, attracting many a wondering eye along the route. Opening the low gate, he stepped hesitantly into the narrow yard and stood eyeing uncertainly the black stone building with its high peaked roof. Two small boys were chasing each other back and forth along the side of the church, and Vankateswami called to them, asking where he could find a priest. He was not sure whether that was the proper term to use, but it was all he knew. They apparently understood, and disappeared immediately behind the building, returning in a few minutes with a short, stocky man of about fifty, whom Vankateswami recognized as the headmaster of the small school next door to the church. He had sometimes come to buy provisions from his uncle Terukalaya.

"Yes?" he intoned, obviously puzzled by the visit of a high-caste Hindu, and the son of a wealthy moneylender at that.

"I want to be a Christian," Vankateswami said, in an effort to get right to the point. "I believe in Jesus—but I haven't done *this* yet." He held out the New Testament he had opened to Mark 16:16 and pointed to that word he didn't understand.

The headmaster's puzzled expression had turned to amazement mixed with unbelief. "*You* want to be baptized?"

"Yes. What does it mean?"

"The priest puts water on your forehead . . . and you join the church. . . . Is that what you want?" His look of unbelief had turned to open astonishment.

Vankateswami nodded. "Whatever that word means, that's what I want to do!"

"I'm only a catechist," he replied apologetically. A smile was beginning cautiously to spread over his face—a look of happiness still
mixed with wonder. "I can't baptize anyone. Only the priest does
that."

"Yes . . . the priest. That's who I asked the boys for. . . ."

"He isn't here. Only comes once a month.

"Oh," Vankateswami half groaned. "I wanted to do it today. Right
now!"

"I'm sorry. Would you like me to call you when he comes next?"

"Yes. Please!"

He had been home less than an hour when a message came that the
priest had arrived unexpectedly and was waiting to see him. Vankateswami hurried from the house and arrived at the chapel in record time,
breathless and excited. A tall, thin man in a long, white robe, which
was tied around the waist, was standing in the doorway of the small
church, talking with the schoolmaster. Looking up when Vankateswami came through the squeaky gate, he smiled at him warmly. His
full beard made him look like a guru.

"Ah, you must be the one," he said in a kind voice. "You want to
be baptized, is that it?"

"Yes! I believe in Jesus, but I haven't done *that* yet, and the Book
says I must."

"That's true . . . but we can't baptize you yet. First you must learn
the Apostles' Creed, the Ten Commandments, the catechism. In
about six months. . . ."

"I'll learn all those things," Vankateswami promised earnestly,
gripping the priest's arm. "But if I should die before six months, then
who will be responsible for my disobedience? No! I must be baptized
now!"

The priest looked like a cornered man. "That would be *very* irregu-
lar. Six months isn't that long."

"I must do what the Book says!" Vankateswami insisted. "Please
don't make me disobey!"

Looking helplessly at the catechist standing open-mouthed beside him, then back at Vankateswami's determined expression, the perplexed priest sighed resignedly and said in a low voice, "All right, I've never done such a thing, but. . . ." He turned to the catechist. "Ring the bell for the congregation to gather. We'll have a baptism!"

And so the rules established by the hierarchy in England were set aside to allow a zealous young man to obey a higher Authority. It was indeed an unorthodox way to join the Church of England—but Vankateswami didn't know he was joining anything. Having turned from the false gods he had served with such poor success for so long, he knew little except that he wanted to obey this Jesus, who was now his Savior and Lord.

The custom was to give former Hindus a Christian name when they were baptized. Because of this young man's unusual zeal, Pastor Joseph named him Paul after the famous apostle. The name meant nothing to Vankateswami. He knew only that he had obeyed the Book and his Lord, and he returned home unspeakably happy.

4

Hinduism Accepts All Religions

It wasn't easy to go back to that church filled with Untouchables, but Vankateswami began to do it regularly every Sunday. As far as he knew, he was the only high-caste Hindu in the whole world who had left his gods to follow Jesus. Sitting in a corner of the small church by himself, he kept his distance from the others, while joining in the prayers and songs. Whether his family knew where he went, or simply didn't care, he wasn't sure; but no one asked any questions.

A number of months after his baptism, while reading the borrowed New Testament aloud with customers and villagers listening, another verse underlined in red caught Vankateswami's attention. He wondered why he hadn't noticed it before. "Therefore if any man be in Christ, he is a new creature: old things are passed away; behold, all things are become new" (2 Corinthians 5:17). Later as he worked on the records he pondered that verse, asking himself whether it was true of him. He believed in Jesus—but was he a new person? Looking back he could see that everything had changed. He hadn't stolen a rupee since Jesus had become his Lord, and he no longer had any fear of hell. A peace beyond comprehension seemed to guard him day and night. "I must really be a Christian!" he thought. "My old life is gone. Just like the Book says, I'm a new person!"

Certainly it was too good to keep to himself. He must tell others how they could have eternal life too.

"I've found the salvation I was searching for!" he said eagerly to Jaigee the next morning when he found her sitting in the yard worshiping the sun.

She turned and stared at him coldly. Lately her eyes seemed to be covered with a dull film. Yet at times one could still see the old shrewdness deep within. She spoke sharply. "When one monkey is spoiled, he will spoil all the rest!" Spitting on the ground, she turned back to her sun worship again. Waiting patiently while she repeated over and over, "Om Siva, Om Siva, Om Rama . . . Rama, Rama, Rama," he thought of Jesus' words to his disciples: "When you pray don't use vain repetitions like the heathen, who think they will be heard if they say it enough times" (*see* Matthew 6:7). It pained him to watch her pursue this hopeless ritual. Fingers lately too crippled to write Rama's name, she whispered it and the names of other gods and the syllable *Om* most of the day.

She stopped speaking and turned to blink at him, apparently surprised that he was still standing beside her. "What is spoiled about this monkey?" he asked.

She said nothing, just stared at him disdainfully, so he persisted. "When I failed my studies, kept bad companions, drank, and stole and lied to cover it up . . . wasn't the monkey spoiled then? Are you not happy that I have changed?"

She turned away. "You have joined this low-caste religion!" she said over her shoulder in a contemptuous tone. "Do you think none of us know where you go? It is a disgrace to our family!"

"I do not touch the Untouchables, so I am within the Law of Manu. I sit in a corner by myself far from the others."

"It is their religion you have touched, and that is worse. Contamination of the body is cleansed with one reincarnation, but the diseases of the soul take many lives to cure."

"I have found the true God!" he said earnestly. "I have peace! There is no fear of hell, and you know how I was tormented by that." He touched her arm gently. "Jaigee, there is salvation without writing Rama's name 100 million times. The true God, Jesus, died for our sins. Believe in him! There is forgiveness!" His sudden boldness startled him. It was unthinkable that he should speak to her like this, but a wave of pity had swept over him. She was growing weaker every month and must have realized that she would never be able to write Rama's name enough times. He wanted her to have the salvation he had found.

She had begun praying again, "Hare Krishna, hare Rama . . . ," louder now, her face uplifted to the sun, and he knew that further conversation was futile. Why had she become so angry? She herself had told him many times how very tolerant Hinduism was of all religions.

Jaigee had not wanted to hear . . . but were there not many others in the village who were anxiously seeking salvation? He did not know of anyone who had really found the peace he sought through temple ritual. He must try to tell them the good news that had changed his life. "This is a faithful saying . . . Christ Jesus came into the world *to save sinners!*"

Since he had first heard of salvation for sinners from someone preaching in the streets, he assumed that this was the proper way to tell others. The day after Jaigee had rebuffed him, when nothing was happening in the business and his figures were up to date, he took the New Testament outside and stood in front of the house facing the open square and began to sing loudly a hymn he had learned at the little church. In no time a crowd of curious villagers had gathered. He opened the Book, read the first fourteen verses in John's Gospel, and began to explain what it meant.

There seemed to be little response either for or against what he was saying, judging from the passive expressions among his listeners. Feeling inadequate to explain the Bible as the missionary had done, Vankateswami told what had happened to him personally: how he had tried everything in Hinduism without finding peace, and how Jesus had saved him. Suddenly a burly farmer from the adjacent Sudra community stepped out of the crowd and grabbed him roughly by the arm.

"We don't want the god of the Untouchables!" he yelled, hitting Vankateswami in the face. No one made a move to intervene, and Vankateswami did not resist. Wasn't this what Jesus said would happen? "Go live with the Untouchables where you belong!" the farmer screamed, hammering more blows that knocked him to the ground.

"Stop!" Half conscious, he heard his father's loud voice shouting. "Get away from him!"

Turning painfully toward the house, Vankateswami saw his father pushing his way through the crowd, followed closely by two of his uncles, and he became aware that his attacker had fled.

"No more talk of this Jesus! Do you hear?" Vankateswami's mother was daubing at his bleeding nose with a damp cloth, while his father paced angrily back and forth, speaking sternly. "You have disgraced the Gupta name! If you want to stay in this house, you must never do again what you did today. Do you understand?"

Vankateswami nodded. "I understand, father."

For several days a battle raged in Vankateswami's conscience. He ought to obey his father . . . but he also ought to tell everyone about Jesus so they could have their sins forgiven too. In an unexpected way, a few days later, the decision was taken out of his hands.

He had gone to the Sudra community just outside the Port Gate early in the morning to get milk. Suffering from a high fever, the dairyman's wife was so weak that she could hardly get out of bed to bring him the milk. "You are sick?" he asked with great concern when she came with the pail full. "I see fever burning in your cheeks."

"Yes, it came upon me last night and it's much worse today."

"I know someone who heals the sick!" he said eagerly without thinking. Only the day before he had read aloud from the New Testament how Peter's mother-in-law had been ill with a high fever, and Jesus had healed her.

Putting a hand upon her forehead, Vankateswami prayed a simple prayer. "Lord Jesus, this woman has a fever just like Peter's mother-in-law had. Please, Lord, show her your love by healing her too. Amen."

"I'm well!" she exclaimed, beginning to laugh with joy. "Husband!" she called loudly. "Come here! I'm well! The gods have healed me!"

"It was not the gods," Vankateswami replied quickly. "There is only one true God, the Creator of us all. He came to this earth as a man to die for our sins. His name is Jesus. He came out of the grave and is alive today. He healed you. Give thanks to him!"

Within hours the news of this miracle had spread through the village. The sick began coming to Vankateswami for prayer, and were healed. Wherever he went in the village, people crowded around asking questions about this god Jesus who could heal the sick. Vankateswami found himself preaching in front of his house again, and on other streets in the village. When Pastor Joseph made his next monthly visit to the nearby chapel, Vankateswami had a surprise for him. About twenty-five Sudras wanted to be baptized. The congregation sat in silent awe watching Pastor Joseph, himself an Untouchable, touch his wet fingers to the Sudras' foreheads, baptizing them in the name of the Father, the Son, and the Holy Spirit.

Feeling a new enthusiasm such as he had not known in years, Pastor Joseph stood talking to Vankateswami long after everyone else had gone. "Next week I'm going to visit another village nearby. You must come with me and we will preach there too. Many Sudras live there. They will listen to you more than to me because of your caste."

Vankateswami was pleased. "Yes, I would like to go. My heart is bursting to tell everyone what Jesus has done for me!"

With deep gratitude Vankateswami told in the next village how the Hindu gods and sacred writings had given him no help, his life had only grown more sinful and empty . . . how he then had found the true God who had died for his sins, and was now forgiven and had the peace he had sought for so long. About thirty Sudras in that village believed, and they, too, were baptized by Pastor Joseph.

"Why must you tell everyone about this Jesus?"

Vankateswami had been so absorbed in his work that he hadn't heard his father come in from the street. Now he looked up from the books, startled by the anger in his voice.

"Is it not enough that you yourself have stooped to take the Untouchables' religion? Must you persuade others to do the same?"

"I have found the salvation that all men seek, father. How can I keep this good news to myself?"

"You do not go to the temples anymore. It is said in the village that you despise Rama and Siva and call them false gods."

"I do not despise those who worship them. But they are all false gods—for they cannot even move but must be carried everywhere . . . so how can they help others, when they cannot help themselves?"

"Stop! You blaspheme the gods! They are all Brahman!"

"If I blaspheme, then let the gods judge me—but they cannot. I am not afraid of them. I have found salvation in Jesus, the true God."

"Jesus is the God of the Untouchables. He's not for *our* caste!"

"He is for everyone, because he is the *only* Savior!"

A sadness had come into his father's voice. "I remember you well as a child upon my knees, when I first told you the story of Hanuman rescuing Rama's wife and you clapped your hands, exclaiming how beautiful a tale it was. Now look at you, forsaking the gods that Hindus have always worshiped!"

Looking around, Vankateswami saw his mother and Jaigee standing in the doorway. His uncles had stopped talking to their customers. Everyone was watching and listening. "You know the devotion I have always had for the gods," he replied earnestly. "The pilgrimages I have made, how regular I was at the temples. But the gods did not help me. Nor did I find salvation in our sacred writings. You know how I read the Bhagavad-Gita aloud. . . ."

"I had hope for you then," his father interrupted.

"But I saw it written there that there is no salvation for sinners . . . yet who else could need salvation? Then I learned that Jesus came to save sinners! Do you not think that was good news?"

"So you go about the streets shouting to everyone to believe in this Jesus. You have taken Sudras to the Untouchables' church, where they have been touched by the leader of the Untouchables! Now I hear that you have gone to another village with this outcaste, riding in the same bullock cart, eating the same food. . . ."

"I have eaten nothing that he has prepared or touched, in spite of the lies that are told. But is there not a change in my life that makes you glad?"

"Glad? Glad to hear the complaint of our relatives that you have brought shame on our name? You have disgraced us all! For *that* I should be glad?"

"I do not steal anymore!" Vankateswami replied softly but earnestly. "Search the books. Add every column of figures. You know that I no longer steal!"

"You never took much. . . ."

"But it was stealing. Are you not glad that I have changed? That I no longer lie to you? The fear of hell that tormented me day and night is gone. I have peace. My sins have been forgiven. Should I not tell others how they can have this peace too?"

"No, you must not! I have warned you before—stop talking about this Jesus or leave the house!"

That was an order Vankateswami found impossible to obey. Whatever the consequence, he must tell everyone who would listen about the salvation he had found, the peace with God, the joy of knowing that his sins were forgiven and that heaven was his home. There were more angry warnings from his father, but they came less frequently, and gradually his family seemed to accept with a certain fatalistic resignation what they called his new religion. Some of the relatives said it was his karma: for having mistreated Christians in his past life, he had been destined to suffer as one of them.

He continued to keep the books for the business. No one tried any longer to persuade him to join in the family puja. There seemed to be less tension . . . and then one morning he was not called to breakfast. Others were told to eat, but he was not. Perhaps it had been an oversight. The family custom was very clear that everyone was to be invited. He said nothing. But at noon the same thing happened. Now Vankateswami realized that he was purposely being excluded. The family also ate supper without him; and that night he wept softly in his bed before falling asleep. When he had disgraced the family by his conduct at high school, and even when he stole from his father, they still had loved and forgiven him. But now that he no longer stole nor drank nor told lies, and had become the kind of son he thought his father had always wanted . . . they seemed to hate him. Yet it was always said that Hinduism, unlike Islam, accepted all religions. Then why did his family seem to hate him for becoming a Christian?

When he was not called for breakfast the next morning, Vankateswami took his New Testament and walked sadly out through the village gate, down the dirt road, then across the paddy fields by a narrow path to a low hill half a mile away. It was covered with dwarf trees and thick, scrubby brush. In a small clearing he found a pile of baked mud on which the farmers placed their ovens when they cooked the saffron that was planted every few years for crop rotation. Sitting there without shade, he read the New Testament, gazing now and then across the fields to his village where he could just make out the roof of his house near the gate. Often during the day as he prayed, his eyes filled with tears. It was devastating to be rejected. Far better to face angry threats than to be ignored.

Returning before supper, he waited in vain to be called. The family ate without him. Breakfast and lunch were the same again the next day. Sitting on that pile of baked mud most of the afternoon, Vankateswami read that Jesus had said, "I came not to bring peace, but a sword. And a man's enemies shall be those of his own household . . . he that loves father and mother more than me is not worthy of me . . . except a man deny himself, take up his cross and follow me he cannot be my disciple" (*see* Matthew 10:34–39). The words on the page blurred, and he wept.

As the sun grew lower on the horizon the evening breeze flipped the pages to Romans, chapter 8. Verse 32 seemed to be a promise from God directly to him: "He that spared not his own Son, but delivered him up for us all, how shall he not with him also freely give us all things?" Why should he fear? God would supply every need. Could he ask more than that? Feeling comforted and strengthened, he made his way slowly back across the fields. Going directly into his room, he knelt beside his bed and quietly thanked God again that he was in his hands.

"Shh! I must tell you something!"

Turning at the voice, Vankateswami saw his uncle Bawala leaning over him, a finger across his lips. He had not heard him enter.

"They will ask you to eat tonight," he whispered, "but *don't do it.* Your life is in danger!" Turning quickly, he tiptoed from the room.

Staggered by what he had just heard, Vankateswami felt suddenly numb. Did they intend to poison him? If they believed what Krishna had told Arjuna, then it was not wrong to take his life—it would just be spinning the wheel of reincarnation, and he would come up again in a new body to make a fresh start toward oneness with Brahman. Still it was hard to believe that his own family would want to *kill* him!

He heard his mother calling other members of the joint family to the table; and then familiar footsteps padded softly into his room. It was Jaigee. Palms together in front of her face, she bowed in the characteristic Hindu greeting when he looked up. "You have not eaten for a long time," she said with apparent concern. "Please come to supper."

"Tell my father I'm not eating tonight," Vankateswami replied quickly.

She hesitated in the doorway. "But this is the third day you have not eaten!"

"I have not been called—but tonight I shall not eat."

She bowed again and left. Soon he heard the heavy, resolute footsteps of his father entering the room, followed by others. Vankateswami didn't look up until his father spoke.

"You do not wish to eat?"

"No, father, not tonight."

"If you will not eat in this house, then you must go!" He had made that threat before under different circumstances, yet it had not been carried out. This time, however, his father was pointing toward the door leading to the porch and street, and it was obvious that he meant what he had said.

"You mean . . . I must leave . . . right *now?*" Vankateswami asked in a weak voice, unable to believe it.

"You have brought this low-caste god into our house. You have disgraced your family. The relatives complain. You refuse to change."

"I have changed, father, for the better."

"Don't mock me! If you don't eat, you must go. Will you eat with us tonight?"

Bawala's words were still echoing: *"Don't eat—*your life is in danger!" Slowly Vankateswami shook his head.

"Then *go! Now!*"

Vankateswami seemed frozen to the bed, too stunned to move or think. Almost audibly he heard the promise again: "He that spared not his own Son, but delivered him up for us all, how shall he not with him also freely give us all things?" God would take care of him. Feeling new strength, he stood to his feet.

With tears streaming from his eyes, he looked at the family facing him from across the room. His mother was just behind his father, an anxious expression on her face. Jaigee was next to her, staring blankly. His uncles and their wives and his brother were near the far door, watching him as though he were some rare species. Looking from one to the other, Vankateswami felt his heart must break. How he loved his family! But they were telling him to leave. He could see that single purpose in every eye. His mother was beginning to cry softly, wiping her face on a corner of her sari: but he knew she agreed with what her husband was doing.

"I love you very much," he said, looking into each face. "But I cannot deny that Jesus is the true God, the Savior of sinners. If for that I must go. . . ." His voice broke and he had to turn away.

When he had regained control of himself, he looked directly into his father's angry eyes and said in a clear voice, "I would rather have Jesus than all of your riches!"

"It's your karma," said his father grimly, pointing to the front door. "It's your karma!"

His mother's sobs grew louder as Vankateswami walked slowly through the living room onto the porch where the business was conducted, then down the steps to the street. In the middle of the small square he paused and looked back. He could see no one peering out of the house. It was dark and the streets were empty. Where should he go? The only possessions he had with him were the dhoti skirt and shirt he wore and the borrowed New Testament clutched tightly in one hand.

It was fourteen miles to Jaigee's brother's house, where he had lived during those two years of high school, but he could be sure of a welcome there. There was an unwritten law that said when a child couldn't get along with its parents, the grandparents would take it in and keep it until the storm passed. It helped him to keep going, knowing that he had always been their favorite. Weak from hunger, slowly he made his way along the dirt road through the Untouchables' village and out to the paved highway that it joined six miles beyond: then eight more miles to Proddutar. Step after exhausted step, with his last bit of strength, he pushed on through its deserted streets to the house he knew so well. The door was locked, for it was after midnight. He knocked and waited. Already he could taste the meal they would give him and feel the comfort of the familiar bed. He knocked again, louder.

It seemed an eternity, but at last he heard footsteps. The voice of Jaigee's brother, half asleep, came muffled through the thick door. "Who's there?"

"It's Vankateswami!" he called back in a happy whisper. "Let me in!"

What a welcome sound to hear the latch being pulled! But the door opened only a crack. He could dimly see his granduncle peering out. "We know all about you! You're not welcome here!" The door was slammed shut and the latch shoved into place.

For a long time Vankateswami stood motionless, senses reeling, the angry voice still ringing in his ears. Fourteen painfully weary miles for *this!* Trembling legs carried him back to the dark street, moving mechanically now. Which way? It was a meaningless question.

"He that spared not his own Son . . . how shall he not with him also freely give us all things?" That promise had given him strength all night. Could he believe it any longer?

"Father! Help me! O my God!" The anguished words were vomited out with a sob.

5

Echoes From the Past

"Paul! Paul!"

Trudging wearily, his eyes downcast, Vankateswami was startled by the voice and looked up to see Pastor Joseph approaching on a bullock cart.

"Paul, my son!" the pastor exclaimed again as the cart drew closer. "I came to look for you!"

"I was on my way to find *you!*" said Vankateswami, sighing with relief as he climbed up beside him, while the driver turned the cart around. "You are my only friend in this world!"

"I heard that your parents put you out," said Pastor Joseph sympathetically. "I'm sorry."

"My relatives won't have me either. Not even my grandparents, where I once lived. By God's grace a boy I knew in high school gave me some food and a bed . . . but this morning his parents told me to leave. They wanted nothing to do with a Christian. . . ."

Pastor Joseph was shaking his head sorrowfully. "I was afraid this would happen. Yet it puzzles me. It is always said that Hinduism is very liberal, accepting all religions . . . but let someone like yourself believe in Christ and there is no more talk of being magnanimous. I know of some who have been killed by their families. Nearly all have to leave their homes."

"I am not certain, but I think they tried to poison me." Vankateswami spoke painfully. It was shattering to admit this about one's own family.

The two sat in uncomfortable silence while the bullock cart bumped and swayed along the road, and the occasional harsh cawings of a crow in the distance called attention to the quiet. It was the pastor who finally spoke—very slowly while he stroked his beard thoughtfully. "I think it would be best that you don't stay in my house."

The slashing stroke of a sword could not have cut deeper. "You . . . don't want . . . me either?" Vankateswami stammered.

"Oh, you misunderstood me!" said the pastor quickly. "I was only thinking . . . if your family would take you back, perhaps in time they would believe in Christ too. But I am an Untouchable. If you live in my house they would *never* have you again!"

"You have much wisdom," responded Vankateswami thoughtfully, nodding his head in rhythm with the swaying cart. "May God grant me to return. My heart aches for my family!"

"No one need know that you stay with me tonight," said the pastor, sounding like a man who has just come to an important decision. "Tomorrow I will find a place for you in the town. Your family comes there often on business. They will see you and talk to you . . . and perhaps take you back, if it is God's will."

They were nearing the pastor's house when he put his hand gently on Vankateswami's shoulder. "There is something I have wanted to say . . . but I did not wish to offend you."

"What is it?"

"You have noticed that I never call you Vankateswami. I do not wish to call you by the name of a Hindu god. Your new name is Paul —and now that you are beginning a new life in a new town and will be making new friends, it would be best that they know you by your Christian name, not the Hindu one."

Vankateswami sat quietly. At last he said, "You are right. I am a new person in Christ. The name my parents gave me belongs to a past life."

"Then I shall introduce you as Paul to my family—and in the town."

"I will be pleased," said Paul, and for the first time that day he began to smile.

For the next nine months Paul made his home on the main street near the edge of town in the small but adequate room Pastor Joseph rented for him the following day. Although he knew that his father or an uncle came into town on business at least once a week, he never saw any of them again. Paul wrote regularly to his parents, telling them where he was living, what he was doing, how much he loved them and wanted to see them . . . but he never received a reply to any of his letters. It was as though the family he had lived with for eighteen years had ceased to exist.

The rented room had no windows, and the only door opened directly onto the busy street. Paul put his cot just outside the door each night to escape the oppressive heat absorbed from the sun by the thin black rocks that formed the roof over the open teak beams. The walls and floor were of the same cut stone, available cheaply from nearby quarries, for which the area was famous. Water had to be carried in a bucket from a public tap a few yards away in the street. It was a drastic change from the large house and comparative luxury he had been used to, but Paul was thankful for a room to call his own and shelter from the monsoon rains when they came. Best of all it was a place where he could study his beloved New Testament undisturbed and spend long hours in prayer. That habit developed in these formative months would build a faith that would eventually carry him around the world on an incredible mission.

After an early breakfast in a restaurant—Pastor Joseph provided the money for his meals—Paul would walk to the large open market nearby where the farmers squatted on the bare earth beside their displays of fresh produce brought in every morning by bullock cart, bicycle, and on foot: squashes, green and yellow beans, peppers, chilies, bitter herbs, cucumbers, tomatoes, potatoes, onions, garlic, and of course rice and other grains. Shoppers would come and go most of the morning in a steady stream across a low bridge leading from the road over a shallow ditch to the market area. Holding his New Testament and a hymnal, Paul would stand on the bridge and begin to sing. When a crowd had gathered, he would read a few verses of Scripture and explain the meaning in a way Hindus could understand. Often he preached from the same verse that had first arrested his attention: "This is a faithful saying, and worthy of all acceptation, that Christ Jesus came into the world to save sinners . . ." (1 Timothy 1:15).

There were always a few sincere seekers who wanted to receive Christ—and others who would stand around arguing in an attempt to prove that Jesus was just one of many gods, *a* way but not *the* way. These sometimes heated discussions were like a fire in which Paul's faith was being tested, tempered, and strengthened. During the long hours he now had for study, sitting on his cot in late afternoon just outside his door beside the road, Paul had an opportunity to make a careful comparison between the Bible and the teachings of Hinduism. The differences were important and many.

Ramakrishna and Vivekananda were among the great Hindu Masters Paul had revered. Teaching that Christ was just one of many avatars, they had popularized the idea that all religions were equally acceptable ways leading to the same place. As Paul studied the New Testament for himself he could see that Christ was not only *the* way, but he led to a different destination: the heaven of the Bible was not the nirvana of Hinduism and Buddhism. The conscious experience of eternal love and joy in God's presence promised by Jesus was diametrically opposed to the idea of losing one's personal existence through being absorbed into the Absolute as a drop of water is absorbed into the ocean. The personal God of the Bible had made everything, but in Hinduism everything was God, creation and Creator were one and the same, which meant that good was evil and God was at the same time Satan. No wonder Krishna called himself "the Prince of Demons"! Hinduism taught that all men were God and needed only to realize it: but the Bible taught that men are separated from God by their own self-will. Through receiving Christ they are forgiven and indwelt by God's Spirit, but remain distinct beings, experiencing God's love and presence forever rather than being absorbed into him.

The Hebrew prophets, claiming inspiration from God, foretold that there would be only *one* incarnation of Deity and not many as Hinduism taught. Called the Messiah, he would be born in Bethlehem, rejected by his own nation, Israel, betrayed by one of his followers for thirty pieces of silver, crucified as a criminal, buried in the grave of a rich man, and resurrected the third day. These and many other specific events the prophets foretold had each been flawlessly fulfilled in Jesus, and *in him alone,* giving irrefutable authentication to his claim that he was "*the* way, *the* truth, *the* life." Clearly Rama, Krishna, Buddha, every so-called avatar and ascended Master were all imposters. None of them had died for the sins of the world and risen again.

Paul noticed that the audiences he preached to grew angry as soon as he said that Christ was the *only* way. The fact that salvation was not available anywhere else was plain enough—so why should it be offensive to be told that Christ was the key to all that they were seeking so unsuccessfully? He wondered why Hindus who had found neither forgiveness nor peace in their endless pilgrimages, mantras, holy baths, sacrifices, rituals, would not be happy to hear that there was forgiveness in Christ. Was this insistence upon a variety of ways to heaven—so one could choose the way most appealing to him—a symptom of man's rebellious unwillingness to let God run his own universe? It was not unreasonable for there to be only *one* way to heaven, since it was available to all. Jesus had died for all, and Paul wanted to tell everyone this good news. Many rejected Christ, insisting upon going their own way—but many believed, and Paul brought each one to Pastor Joseph for baptism.

The changed lives of such men and women were always a great encouragement. There were, however, some bitter disappointments, and strangely enough they involved healing, which had seemed such a powerful factor in convincing Hindus in his own village that Christ is the Savior of sinners. Paul had become involved in praying for the sick in this town too. It all began with a farmer who had come from the market to Paul's room to ask about Jesus. He had been unusually thin, and prolonged pain had drawn deep lines in his sallow face. In response to Paul's sympathetic question he had made known a serious abdominal problem the doctors had not been able to cure. Paul's prayer for him had brought instant healing. Gratefully he had promised to believe in Christ and to pray only to him. Others, hearing of this, asked for prayer, and they also were healed, which caused more Hindus to turn to Christ.

One evening Paul walked three miles to this farmer's home to visit him. "I haven't seen you in several weeks," Paul said when they had exchanged greetings in front of the low thatched hut.

"I've been too busy lately to stop at your room," came the apologetic reply, but in a tone that made Paul suspect he wasn't telling the whole truth.

"I've missed you—so I walked out here to see how you are. I brought my Bible. We can study it together."

The farmer's wife had appeared in the open doorway and was standing with hands on hips, glaring at Paul with evident disapproval. Her husband began nervously brushing at flies and edged a few steps farther from the hut.

"I don't want to talk about Jesus," he said in a voice too low to reach his wife's straining ears. "We have our own gods."

Paul's mouth dropped open in astonishment. "But you promised to pray to Jesus every day!" he protested.

"I don't need this Jesus now," replied the farmer. "If I get sick again, then I'll pray to him—but we have no image of Jesus among our family gods."

Disappointing experiences like this, of which there were several, made Paul realize that many people wanted Christ to save them from illness and pain, and of course from hell, but not from their sins. They didn't want him to interfere with their lives. It was a sad day when he learned from Pastor Joseph that the Sudras he had baptized in his own village, many of whom had been healed, were not coming to the church because they didn't want to associate with Untouchables.

Then came an even more severe test of Paul's faith. He fell seriously ill himself, and though he prayed earnestly, he only grew worse. Intense stomach pains, nausea, and violent vomiting made it impossible for him to leave his room. Daily he grew weaker. Pastor Joseph found him lying on his cot soaked with sweat, his eyes like fire smoldering in two sunken craters.

"You should be in the hospital!" the pastor exclaimed.

"I have prayed for others and they have been healed," moaned Paul in semidelirium. "For days I have prayed for myself, and I only grow worse. Has God forgotten me?"

"He has not forgotten you!" replied the pastor quickly. "You are being tested. Do not lose faith!" He reached down and half lifted Paul from the cot. "Now put your arm around my neck and lean on me. We're going to the mission hospital—it isn't far."

When he was discharged ten days later, still weak but on the mend, the pastor took him into his own home, since there had been no indication that his family would ever be willing to take him back. Shortly after Paul came to live with him, Pastor Joseph was given a more important assignment in another town, and Paul, who was treated by the entire family as though he were one of them, moved with them.

Paul was now nineteen. More than a year had passed since he'd been put out of his parents' home. That had been a black night full of fear and despair, and there had been disappointments and times of uncertainty since—but looking back he could see God's hand guiding and providing all of the way. That verse in Romans—"He that spared not his own Son . . . how shall he not with him also freely give us all things?"—had been proved true countless times. He still owned nothing more than a Bible and the clothes he had been wearing when he had left home; but he had lacked for nothing, and he was convinced that he never would. Though deficient in theological training, Paul was learning to walk with his heavenly Father and to trust him for each step along the way.

In charge of an even larger district now that included about forty churches, Pastor Joseph took Paul with him everywhere as he made his rounds from village to village on the bullock cart. Bullocks walk very deliberately, and during the many hours they spent together on the cart the pastor taught Paul as much as he could from the Bible. It was during these invaluable lessons that Paul first learned something about Christians that shocked him.

"You think that everyone who attends the churches we visit is a Christian," said Pastor Joseph one day. "Although they call themselves Christians, many of them aren't—and in some churches most of the congregation, including even the pastor, are unsaved."

"You mean they still worship the Hindu gods?" asked Paul.

"Oh, no. Most of them come from families that have called themselves Christians for centuries, some as far back as when Saint Thomas visited India. They have nothing to do with Hinduism."

"Then why do you say they aren't real Christians?"

"They have a relationship with the church, but no personal relationship with Christ. They have never been born again."

"But they've been baptized, and they call themselves Christians!" Paul protested. "They attend church and repeat the prayers and the creed!"

"So they do—but it's only a habit learned in childhood. The prayers and creed are just words that come from their mouths, and perhaps even from their heads, but not from their hearts. Never having repented of their sin and personally received Christ into their hearts as Lord and Savior, such people are as lost as any Hindu who thinks Jesus is just another god."

"This is a surprise to me," said Paul sadly, and lapsed into a long, thoughtful silence. How could he dare to tell people who thought they were Christians that they needed to repent of their sin and receive Christ?

The pastor seemed to know his thoughts. "God has called you to be an evangelist. And you must preach salvation not only to Hindus but in the churches to those who think they are Christians. Don't ever forget that!"

So impressed were church officials by Paul's evangelistic talents that he was sent to school to become a priest. Much of the time was devoted to learning what prayers to read for what occasion, when to kneel down and when to stand up, when to face the congregation and when to face the altar. It reminded him of the Hindu rituals he had ridiculed as a boy. He could not believe that the Creator of the universe was impressed by special robes, motions, and postures. Each day he seemed to hear a little louder an echo from the past that troubled him and made the rituals he was learning increasingly distasteful.

During a brief holiday, Paul was invited to a conference of church catechists to tell them how he, a high-caste Hindu, had become a Christian. "Be sure to explain what it means to know Christ personally!" Pastor Joseph had reminded him. Paul did his best—and so did another speaker who preached salvation more clearly and powerfully than Paul had ever heard. Extremely large for an Indian, tall and heavy, with the strange name of Agrippa, this "layman," as he was called, seemed to know the Bible far better than any catechist, priest, or bishop Paul had ever met. Unlike the priests, who usually read everything, this dynamic preacher spoke rapidly without notes, and with a persuasive power such as Paul had never encountered in his life. Every argument was backed up with verse after verse of Scripture, from Genesis to Revelation, which Agrippa seemed to have memorized and indexed in his mind for instant recall when needed. On his lips the Bible was a razor-sharp sword that pierced the heart and cut away everything superfluous, leaving one with the feeling of being naked like Adam and Eve under the searching gaze of a holy God.

"I must go with you!" Paul said to Agrippa, when the latter had to leave to conduct meetings elsewhere. "God has spoken to me through your words. You've set my heart on fire, and I must hear more!"

"Don't be impulsive . . . you have your studies to finish," Agrippa cautioned him; but there was an approving gleam in his eye. He liked what he'd learned of this young Hindu convert in their brief conversations together.

Through the billowing clouds of dust rising from the wheels of the bullock cart that took Agrippa from the conference grounds that hot day, Paul could be seen sitting beside him, the two of them talking earnestly together as they receded into the distance. It was the beginning of a new adventure for Paul, and of a deeper relationship with Christ, who seemed to be living in this man. Hindus noticed this, too, and Paul was astonished to see thousands gather to hear Agrippa wherever he went. God seemed to talk to men with Agrippa's voice. Many would break down in tears, weeping over lives of rebellion, repenting of their sins, receiving Christ as Lord and Savior. Paul would weep, too, his heart burning with the desire to know Christ as Agrippa knew him, and to be able to preach Christ to the world with that power of God's Spirit that so obviously exploded in every word of this simple, uneducated "layman." Far better to learn from him how to win souls than to spend months learning the rituals to be performed as a parish priest.

Agrippa baptized his converts on the spot if there was enough water available—in a river, well, or any pool deep enough. The manner of baptism astonished Paul—no wet hand on foreheads, but complete immersion under the water.

"Why do you baptize this way?" Paul asked.

"Because baptism is a picture of dying and being buried with Christ and rising again in new life. You don't splash a few clods of dirt on a dead man—you bury him." And to back up what he had said, Agrippa quoted every verse about baptism in the New Testament.

Paul was convinced. "I want to be baptized that way, too!"

Agrippa was silent for a moment, studying Paul's eyes. "They'll put you out of your church," he said at last, a touch of sadness in his voice.

"Out of the church?" Paul exclaimed.

Agrippa nodded. "I'm sorry. Christians sometimes quarrel about things like baptism. You might as well learn that now."

Paul had made up his mind. "I want to follow Jesus, not a church!" he said resolutely.

"Where have you been?" Pastor Joseph asked Paul accusingly when at last he returned home.

"I have been traveling with a powerful evangelist!" Paul replied enthusiastically. "What an experience! I learned more about evangelism by listening to him than I could ever learn at the school."

"Yes, the school," said the pastor, narrowing his eyes. "They said you'd disappeared. . . ."

"I don't believe God wants me to be a parish priest. You yourself said I was called to be an evangelist!"

"Who was this man you were with?"

"They call him Agrippa."

The pastor's face darkened. "Agrippa is a dangerous man," he said with an unhappy scowl. "If you're not careful he'll baptize you in a river, or a well—shove you right under!"

"But what's wrong with that?" Paul asked. "He baptized me too!"

"Did you forget that *I* had already baptized you?" demanded the pastor in a hurt voice, fixing Paul with an indignant eye.

"Just a few drops on the head, but the Bible says. . . ."

"So you despise the baptism of the church!"

"I don't despise it. . . ." Feeling helplessly bewildered, Paul seemed to hear another echo from the past. It frightened him, and he turned away to hide his trembling lip.

"You have been like a son to me," said Pastor Joseph. Sorrow and anger were mingled together in his voice. He seemed to choke. When he began speaking again the anger had gained control. "You have proved your unworthiness either to remain in the church . . . or in my house. Please leave as soon as possible!"

The echoes from the past grew louder, until Paul thought his head would burst with the discordant sound.

6

Never! Never!

Taken into the house of a Mr. Daniel in Madras, Paul soon learned that here was another remarkable man whom God had brought into his life for a purpose. Having worked with Intervarsity Christian Fellowship for years, holding meetings at many universities, he had founded the Laymen's Evangelical Fellowship to train recent graduates in the Word of God and to help place them in key positions in business and government. Living by faith, he was a man of prayer who expected miracles from God. Some of the vital spiritual principals Paul had already begun to learn were strengthened and clarified under the training he received from this godly man. Although Mr. Daniel normally took young men in for only six months, Paul lived nearly two years in his home, daily preaching in the streets of Madras and handing out Gospels of John as he walked back and forth across that great city.

Learning that there were many villages where Christ had never been preached around Anantapur, a district headquarters in the center of southern India, Paul spent much time there beginning in 1940, traveling sometimes alone, sometimes with Agrippa and a young Hindu convert named Probuddas, who became like a brother to him. Paul often preached in churches, but best of all he loved to preach Christ to the Hindus in the streets. In his travels he sometimes encountered cases of demon possession similar to those he had seen as a boy. Hindus commonly believed that such people had been "possessed" by one of the gods. The god would leave only when friends and relatives had promised great sacrifices to it. Now Paul realized that these gods actually represented demons, who used the idols to control those who worshiped them. Having read in the Scriptures that Jesus cast out demons, Paul began to do the same in His name.

In one village he was called by a pastor's wife to deliver a Hindu woman who was possessed. She was an uneducated coolie with little intelligence, yet when he commanded the demon to come out of her she made a lengthy objection in perfect English, a language she didn't know. When the devil was cast out, the woman could speak only in her own dialect again. The ability to speak, under hypnosis, in languages one didn't normally know was supposed to prove reincarnation. Presumably the language had been learned in a previous life. Paul knew this was a lie of Satan, having cast out demons responsible for such phenomena. He was learning that the Christian's warfare is not against flesh and blood, but against spiritual powers of evil.

The arrival of Bakt Singh turned the churches of Madras upside down. Upset because their members, who were nearly all nominal Christians, were being converted by the thousands through his preaching, pastors closed their pulpits to Bakt Singh. So crowds gathered in the open air, as many as twelve thousand on one occasion, to hear this man of God preach. Many seriously ill were healed when Bakt Singh prayed for them, even deaf and dumb began to hear and speak. Paul's heart was deeply stirred by his preaching, and from the moment they met there was an immediate bond between these two former Hindus. Becoming a Telugu interpreter at Bakt Singh's meetings, Paul learned much about preaching by repeating this powerful evangelist's sermons after him. Here was another man of faith and prayer who trusted God for everything. Paul was deeply influenced by his life and teaching, and lived for a time at Jehovah Shamah, a large house on several acres of land that Bakt Singh's associates had purchased in Madras. There were constant meetings and crowds of four and five thousand often gathered in the open field next to the house.

While staying at Jehovah Shamah, Paul met Dr. Raju, a former medical doctor turned evangelist, who was to have a unique influence upon his future life.

Since Dr. Raju also spoke Telugu, he and Paul were naturally drawn to each other when the doctor first visited Jehovah Shamah, and soon they became close friends. As a result, Dr. Raju invited Paul to preach in the Brethren Assembly in Narsapur, about 200 miles north of Madras, where he was an elder, and soon Paul was preaching there regularly, always staying with the Raju family.

The one person who had the deepest spiritual influence upon Paul was Silas Fox, a Canadian missionary who had come to India years before. Known among Hindus as the "White Brahmin," Fox was about sixty years old when Paul met him, but looked much younger. An unforgettable man in many ways, he would arise at 4:30 for calisthenics, as well as prayer and Bible study, and often stood on his head, which he said helped the circulation in his brain. Whether that was the secret or not, he had a remarkable mind and could speak six or seven Indian languages, including Hindi and Sanskrit, better than those who had learned them as their mother tongue. That was reason enough for the Indians to flock to hear him—but he had that same power of the Holy Spirit that marked his close friend Agrippa's preaching, and crowds would gather wherever he went. This man of God, who gave so many decades of his life to India, took a deep personal interest in Paul, and during the next six years spent many hours teaching him from the Scriptures day after day whenever they were together, which was often for weeks at a time.

Paul sometimes traveled from village to village as an apprentice evangelist with Fox and Agrippa—now and then accompanied by Dr. Raju. About five years after he had been turned away from his grandfather's door, Paul had the great joy of returning with these three men to Proddutar to preach the Gospel. Every evening for a week they held an outdoor meeting in the center of town in front of the Rama temple. Filling the temple porch and the street, the crowds spilled over onto the steps of Jaigee's brother's place of business and onto the porch of a large Moslem shop. Before the "White Brahmin" would deliver the main sermon of the evening, a Hindu convert from each of the castes —Brahmin, Kshatriya, Vaisya, and Sudra—would tell how he became a follower of the Lord Jesus Christ. Paul spoke for the Vaisyas, the predominant caste in Proddutar. The town was filled with his relatives, all very antagonistic, except for one cousin who gave him the latest news of his family. Paul had not heard a word of response from them, although he continued to write regularly, pleading with them to receive Christ. According to his cousin, his mother and father were both well; so were his uncles, but Jaigee was very feeble and not expected to live long. The business was not prospering as it once had. The entire Vaisya village that Paul had grown up in was experiencing difficult times. Only the Christians in the Untouchables' village seemed to be flourishing.

In this town that had witnessed his defeated life of debauchery and failure at school, Paul now went daily from door to door inviting people to the evening meetings and telling everyone about the victory he had found in Christ. A number of Hindus received Christ during this week, among them one of Paul's cousins. At his baptism he also wanted the name "Paul." He became such a joyful person after receiving Christ, that everyone started to call him "Happy Paul," and that name stuck. He, too, became a traveling evangelist.

Whenever Paul came to Narsapur to preach he always stayed in the Raju home. The eldest daughter, Devi, a beautiful and deeply spiritual girl, attracted his attention from the start. Because she had excellent penmanship and knew her grammar well, while Paul had not finished high school, Devi wrote many letters for him in response to the mail he was now receiving from all over India. This was their only contact, for it would have been very improper for an unmarried man and woman to spend any time alone in conversation. As he dictated letters to this shy and proper girl, answered her hesitant and softly spoken questions when his meaning wasn't clear, and watched her write his letters in perfect form, Paul came to admire Devi.

For some time it had been apparent to Paul that he needed a wife to help in his ministry. There were many women, some of them unmarried, who came forward for salvation and counseling in his meetings, and it was difficult for him to help them when the customs were so firmly against unmarried men speaking with women. As Paul prayed about this need, he became convinced that the Lord had chosen Devi Raju for his wife. But she came from a wealthy family. Her father owned land and her mother had a lucrative lace business, and all of the relatives were very wealthy. He had no job, no income, no property—nothing that was customary to commend a man to the parents of such a girl. In spite of this he found the courage one day to approach Dr. Raju about marrying Devi. Any discussion of marriage should have been conducted by Paul's parents, but that was impossible. Dr. Raju listened quietly and told Paul that the family would pray about it and let him know.

Leaving this important matter in God's hands, Paul left for Bellary, where he was to conduct a series of meetings.

"You have noticed Paul Gupta?" Devi's grandmother asked her one afternoon when they were sitting together on the back veranda. The air was laden with the scent of roses, Easter lilies, and jasmine growing prolifically in the garden they faced.

"I have noticed him," said Devi in a disinterested tone, lowering her gaze. "How could I help it with the pile of letters I do for him every time he stays with us for a few days!"

"He is a good preacher," her grandmother continued.

"So I have often heard people say."

"And in your opinion . . . ?"

"God has spoken to me when he has preached in our chapel."

"He has approached your father about marrying you. . . ."

Eyes flashing, Devi jumped to her feet and turned to face her grandmother—surprise, disapproval, and dismay combining on her expressive face. Recovering herself, she murmured an apology and sat down.

"Well?" insisted her grandmother. "Would you be willing?"

Sparks were flying from Devi's eyes. "Never!"

"But he is a godly man!"

"He has nothing—no land, no income, no property . . . !"

"But he walks with the Lord . . . I know it in my heart!"

"That isn't the only thing a girl expects in a husband."

"There aren't many caste Christians—they're almost all Untouchables."

Devi tossed her head. *"Almost . . . but not all!"*

"You have had other offers that your father did not approve. Whom would you marry?"

"I have not thought of it," she said in a defensive tone. "I am too young."

"You are eighteen. Many girls are matched up far younger. We are praying about Paul's proposal, and wanted to know your reaction."

"I don't need to pray about *him!*" said Devi warmly, close to tears now. "He has little education, was put out of school I understand, and put out of his home also. . . ."

"And so was I!" interjected her grandmother quickly. "You know the story well, how I had to flee for my life. And so did my husband, who is now with the Lord—and so did your other grandparents. That is nothing to hold against a man. It is something for which the Lord will reward him."

Devi was wiping her eyes now on a corner of her sari. "Please don't talk of him anymore! I could not bear to marry such a man!" Stifling her sobs, she ran into the house and threw herself across her bed, where she lay for a long time crying softly.

Well she knew the unbreakable custom that a girl and boy of marriageable age must resign themselves to whatever match their parents decided upon. But hers were asking her opinion, and she had reason to hope they would not force her against her will. There were so many other more suitable young men whose parents would like to arrange a match with her. Why did her parents favor this penniless preacher? He was not at all like the ideal she and her mother had often discussed. Hadn't she been a good daughter? Wasn't she worth more than *this?* She would *never* marry such a man!

"Never!" she told herself between sobs. "Never! *Never!*"

7

A Partner Chosen by God

The Raju home was large enough to have its own sickroom, with a broad window looking out on the garden, which was hidden from prying eyes by the high, thick brick wall that surrounded the entire property. Devi lay on the bed nearest to the open window, weakly savoring the elusive scent of roses and lilies that drifted into the room on the hot afternoon air that was still heavy with moisture from a passing thundershower. The steady *drip, drip* from the eaves and the dogged rhythm of a coolie scratching his hoe between the long rows of garlic sprouts and wax beans just beyond the flower beds marked the passage of time like the ticking of a clock. Nature and men were going through their monotonous routines all over India in spite of disease and starvation.

The latter had never touched Devi: but the typhoid she had taken a few days after her grandmother's appeal to prayerfully consider Paul Gupta's proposal had brought her to the very gates of death, from which her father's skillful and frantic efforts, and fervent prayers, had barely saved her. For three weeks a raging fever had burned mercilessly through her body, leaving her weakened and emaciated. Today was the first time she had been able to concentrate her thoughts upon this problem that had haunted her through weeks of feverish nightmare. According to her father it would be another two months before she would, by God's grace, have strength enough to walk around in the yard and braid her own long, jet-black hair.

Her eighteen years had all been lived in this house she loved. Every crack in the plastered walls and the open tile roof were as familiar as the taste of the thick, sweet milk that came from the two buffaloes she could hear rattling the wooden bars in their sheds beyond the garden. She thought of other illnesses spent in this room during childhood and marveled that the pain of those past fevers had blended into a nostalgia of happy memories that tore at her heart now as the prospect of marriage faced her. Yes, she *was* too young to leave this home she loved. She would insist upon that.

The familiar sounds of the household and the aroma of spicy chutney cooking in the kitchen overwhelmed her with a bittersweet sense of the past merging into the future. She had been about eight, a saucy but tender girl who loved to play and wouldn't go out of the house without a flower in her sleekly combed hair, when her parents had surrendered their lives to the Lord, and her father had given up his medical practice to preach the Gospel. At first she had resented the changes that decision had brought: rising at 4:30 for family Bible study and prayer together under her father's zealous direction, each member of the household then spending additional time "alone with the Lord" before breakfast. When her father was away preaching, which was soon too often, her mother led the family prayer and taught the children from the Scriptures.

Well she remembered the Sunday afternoon she had committed her own life to Christ. Only ten at the time, sitting on the floor with her brothers, she had been strangely moved as her mother had talked to them about the Second Coming of Christ. Devi had often told her parents that she would be in heaven too, but she would wait until she was dying before accepting Christ at the last moment. Now her mother was warning her children that Christ could come at any time, and when no one expected him. Instantly those who were his own would vanish from the earth. Those who rejected him would be left behind for judgment. There would be no time to accept him at the last moment—it would happen too quickly. All afternoon her mother's plea to receive Christ *now* before it was too late had rung in her ears, but Devi had resisted. She wanted a life of fun and joy, not one of self-denial in following Christ.

That evening when her father returned he had read the Scriptures again with the family—a portion in Isaiah that spoke of the millennium. "My great sorrow," he had said, sounding unusually solemn, "is to think that your mother and I will be in the presence of our Lord enjoying his peace and joy, and perhaps some of our children will not be there with us."

Again the Holy Spirit had pleaded with Devi. Perhaps it had been more out of love for her parents, more wanting to be with them than wanting to follow Jesus—but in her childish way she had asked Christ to be her Lord and Savior. The years that followed had brought a maturity and deepening understanding of that simple act of faith; but in her young mind it had been real enough at the time, and had brought great joy to her parents.

Devi's mother operated a lace business from her home, supplying distributors with fancy handwork. Hindu women came to her regularly to receive yarn and patterns for crocheting in their own homes, which the Kshatriya women rarely leave, guarded as they are from alien eyes almost as jealously as Moslem women. Now that she knew the Savior, Devi urged these women every time they came to her house to believe on Christ also. They would smile at her and tell her that she was much too young to be so concerned about religion. "Our gods are good to us, and your god is good to you," they would say, patting her affectionately, but she would not be put off. No one came into the Raju home without listening to Devi's childish but persuasive sermons.

Such were the memories that swept over her now as she lay recovering from typhoid . . . memories of a youth that had been filled with the joy of being in God's will and service. Now that joy had left her. Only the day before, her grandmother had mentioned Paul again, asked her to pray about him, and she had refused. But she couldn't brush this gentle and godly woman's quiet words out of her thoughts. "We all think the marriage would be God's will," she had said. Devi

The original bungalow on the present property. Door on right leads to quarters Donald Fox and family had occupied, where first printing press was set up. It is now a bookstore. The Gupta family occupies remainder of house. *Below:* The original dormitory on property purchased from Strict Baptist Mission as it looks today after remodelling and expansion. Now used for first year male students.

A typical village crowd listening to students from the Institute preaching the Gospel
which is done every afternoon
as part of their practical evangelism training. *Left:* The first
building constructed. Planned
by Paul to be a thatched hut,
today it contains classrooms, library, and the studio where re-
cordings are made for the radio
broadcasts that now bring a response of about 40,000 letters a
year.

Dining room and kitchen completed in 1962 and still in use although inadequate for present student body. *Below:* A group of women students in 1974 outside the girls' hostel. Completed in 1962, it is now crowded to capacity, limiting the number of girls who can be accepted.

Housing for married students. *Below:* The Gupta family in July 1974. Standing: Ruth, Bobby, Samuel, John and his wife Linda. Seated: Dolly, Dr. Gupta, Mrs. Devi Gupta holding her grandson Jonathan, and Daniel.

Men's dormitory begun in 1970 that used up remaining land. Ground floor contains on the right (hidden by trees) Calvary Memorial Chapel, and on the left the offices of the dean, president, registrar and other administrative staff. In addition to the students' rooms, there are also a small hospital and dispensary on the second floor. *Below:* Partial view of students gathered in Calvary Memorial Chapel.

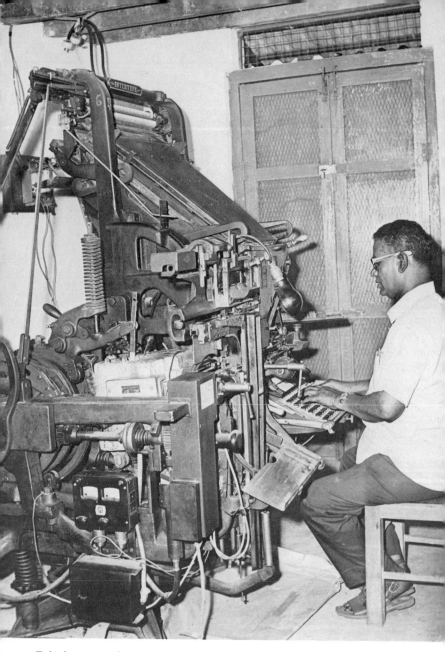

Printing supervisor operating Linotype machine that helps speed publication of millions of copies of Christian literature each year.

Paul preaching to a street crowd through an interpreter (holding microphone) during the December, 1973 Gospel Tour to Kakinada. Instrument on far right is a harmonium. *Below:* A recent graduating class preparing to enter Calvary Memorial Chapel. Married students quarters in left background.

had felt an angry rebellion rising within her, and a terrifying feeling of being cornered. Instinctively she knew it *was* God's will, and that tormented her. She had often told others that because God is perfect in wisdom and love his will is the very best choice for every life; yet now she would not yield to that loving Wisdom. It frightened her to realize that she did not want God's will—not in *this* matter—but still she refused to yield. She would *never* marry Paul Gupta! How could her parents consider such a match? It was beneath them and beneath her!

All that day she seemed to hear the voice of God saying, "You are rejecting *me* by rejecting the man I have chosen for you!" There was no escaping this voice. Devi's head began to throb until she thought it would burst with the pain. Twice the inner struggle came to a climax with the *Never!* she inwardly screamed reaching a crescendo. The third time the frightening realization that she was saying *Never!* to God overwhelmed her. She was not rejecting Paul Gupta but the Lordship of Christ, telling him that in this matter at least she would insist upon her own way. Was that not folly as well as shame? Such rebellion would tear God from his throne, refusing to allow the Creator to run his own universe. Horrified at this sin, she sobbed out her repentance, surrendering to the wisdom and love of her heavenly Father. "Never!" turned to, "Yes, Lord, I will accept your choice for my life."

The wedding announcement was met with mixed feelings at Bethany Gospel Chapel, the large Brethren Assembly in Narsapur where the Rajus attended. Most of the people thought it was a good match. After all, Paul was a man who loved the Lord and one who had learned to trust and follow him. Would he not make a good husband? But some of the closer friends and relatives were indignant and upset. Devi was marrying beneath herself. This young man had nothing. He said the Lord provided for his needs —but was that any way to live, especially with the responsibilities of a wife and family?

Both Paul and Dr. Raju wanted Bakt Singh to perform the marriage, and their letter to him brought an affirmative response. Friends and relatives were unhappy to learn that Bakt Singh insisted upon a simple wedding. No costly sari for the bride, only a plain white cotton suit for the groom, no jewelry or pomp. Dr. and Mrs. Raju were not too happy about that either. A wedding is an important occasion that happens only once in a lifetime. For eighteen years they had looked forward to this and wanted Devi to have the best one possible. It wasn't a sin to wear nice clothes. That was only showing respect for the occasion.

Paul's ministry had touched many lives. Learning of the coming wedding, friends began to shower him with gifts, including a beautiful white sari in Benares silk, traditional for brides, far too expensive for him to afford. He felt guilty accepting it, knowing that Bakt Singh would never allow it. Nevertheless he presented it to Dr. Raju for his daughter—along with gold, also a gift from a friend, to be made into a *thali,* the traditional pendant the groom always ties around the bride's neck, symbolic of their lives being bound together. Bakt Singh wouldn't consent to that either—nor to the traditional navy blue suit that had also been given to Paul. How could these gifts have come from the Lord if they couldn't be used?

The day of the wedding arrived. May 2, 1946. Many of Paul's friends had come two or three hundred miles from all directions. Paul was preparing to dress in a simple white cotton suit and Devi in a plain cotton sari, when a telegram arrived from Bakt Singh stating that he had been called suddenly to England and would not be able to perform the ceremony. Quickly other arrangements were made; and in a few hours Paul, in his blue suit, and Devi, in her white sari of Benares silk, were standing together in Bethany Gospel Chapel in front of more than a thousand guests, being united in holy matrimony. Some of Devi's closest friends were missing because unmarried girls could not attend weddings. One of her great uncles performed the ceremony, and another uncle and Agrippa each preached a sermon, exhorting the bride and groom to follow the Lord and appealing to the many Hindu and Moslem guests to receive Christ. Steadfastly opposed to this match from the beginning, Devi's uncle made it clear to all the guests that the marriage did not have his blessing. "Today we're putting two ships on the sea," he allegorized, "with no protection from the storm, and we don't know where they'll break up in the waves." He looked Devi in the eye when he said it, as though to remind her of his warnings that her husband would not take care of her.

For one frightful moment her faith faltered, she wanted to run down the aisle and out the door back to her room to be a little girl again. Then she reminded herself that this was God's will and she was in his hands. That didn't lessen the embarrassment of wondering how many of the guests there that day agreed with her uncle. How many were hiding the same thoughts behind polite smiles? A quick sidewise glance at Paul told her that he either hadn't noticed the remark or was immune to the opinions of men, intent only upon serving God. She had to dig her fingernails into her palms and bite her lip to hold back the tears, determined not to allow men's ideas to sway her or to rob her of the joy that comes from knowing one has surrendered to the Lord and is in his will.

Representing the groom, Agrippa, a stranger to Devi, preached an answering sermon, far more eloquent and persuasive than her uncle's had been in his appeal to the unbelievers present. Eloquent, too, in his description of the groom as a man of God, a faithful servant of Jesus Christ worthy of the bride's affection and trust. Now Devi had to clench her fists again to keep a broad smile from bursting out all over her face, unbecoming to a proper bride. Agrippa was a man who knew her husband well, and that thought comforted Devi.

Her *husband!* They were standing arm in arm now, as she had often dreamed it would be, facing the guests, who were smiling and looking as though they didn't share her uncle's fears; and Devi knew she was very, very happy. They walked down the aisle as husband and wife. Could it be true? Devi's smile burst out of its prison and her expressive eyes glowed with satisfaction, especially when the long garlands of brilliant flowers were hung around their necks, fragrant and sweet, like the flowers she always wore in her hair as a girl. Those days had slipped forever into the past. Something new was beginning, and it hardly seemed real.

8

Triumph and Tragedy

I have the joy, joy, joy, joy, down in my heart!
Down in my heart, down in my heart!
I have the joy, joy, joy, joy, down in my heart!
Down in my heart to stay!

Hand in hand, singing at the top of their voices, Paul and Devi made the countryside ring with song each afternoon as they climbed the grassy, wooded hill outside of Mercara, a beautiful mountain town near India's southern tip. After prayer on top of the hill, they would return, singing psalms Paul had put to music—hoping a few words would lodge in the heart of a farmer working in an orchard or riding by on a bullock cart, or of a coolie woman with a heavy bundle of sticks on her head steadied by one hand, faded and filthy sari skirt clutched with the other, holding its tattered hem up out of the way of calloused bare feet.

Paul's travels had previously brought him here. The local church, like so many others, had been largely made up of nominal Christians, religious but without a personal relationship to Christ. Paul had made the salvation message clear, just as Pastor Joseph had taught him, and as a result many members of long standing, including the pastor's daughter, had come forward with tears of repentance to receive Christ into their lives, bringing a great transformation to that church. Paul had been invited to come with his bride to spend a month in this cooler mountain climate. The manager of a local bank, a Mr. Amana, who had also become a Christian through Paul's preaching, had arranged for them to stay in a large and comfortable missionary bungalow that was now empty. In a tip'n-carry, the multistoried aluminum food carrier so common all over India, he brought their meals to them twice daily, piping hot, prepared by his mother.

Paul was a man of strong convictions, driven by the desire to win India for Christ. Devi admired him for his passion for lost souls—but it also frightened her. In spite of her surrender to God's will there were times of renewed doubts. With a husband who was always out in the streets preaching all over India, what home could they have? Would they be like nomads, always moving from place to place? Despite these recurring anxieties she was happy. Seeing how God used Paul in others' lives, her respect for him had deepened: and as she experienced his tender concern for her, a response of love was awakened in her own heart.

In addition to preaching in the church every night, Paul visited his converts and taught Bible classes during the day; but he and Devi were still able to spend much time on their knees side by side in prayer. What better way to get to know one another than to bare their hearts together before the Lord? There was much to pray about, but their main concern was for God to reveal what they should do as husband and wife to spread the Gospel across this vast country with one-fifth of the world's population. The lost all over India were on Paul's heart day and night.

While Paul and Devi prayed earnestly for lost souls, the political destiny of India's 400 millions was being debated in Parliament, bartered at Number 10 Downing Street, plotted in maneuvers and countermaneuvers of rival political factions . . . and would in large measure be decided by rioting mobs of Hindus and Moslems massacring each other in the streets of Calcutta, Bombay, Delhi, and villages almost unheard of before, like Srirampur. A dwarfed and ugly man, hardly more than skin and bones because of frequent death fasts, had broken the power of the world's mightiest empire. With his passive resistance campaigns, Mohandas Karamchand Gandhi (who was considered by his enemies to be a shrewd, conniving political opportunist, but was known as Mahatma—"great soul"—and much revered as a saint by his millions of fanatically devoted followers) had forced no less a leader than Winston Churchill to eat his own words. What Churchill had vowed would "never be relinquished" would indeed be given up. British rule in India—nearly three centuries long—was about to end. That much had been settled. When, how, and at what cost in bloodshed were the only questions remaining. *Independence* was a word on every heart and lip, a heady subject for editors and political leaders, a slogan to excite even the lowly coolies with unfounded hopes that for tens of thousands of them would end in sudden, violent death.

Too absorbed in his concern for India's spiritual future to have time to follow the unfolding drama of her political destiny, Paul was nonetheless not blind to what Independence would mean to the Indian Church when it inevitably came. This realization had for some months laid a heavy burden upon him, and painted in his mind what seemed like a wild dream, which he began to share cautiously with Devi as they prayed together for God's guidance.

"The emptiness of this large bungalow speaks to me like the voice of a prophet," Paul remarked one afternoon as they left to climb the hill for prayer. "The foreign missionaries who built it are already gone, even before Independence. But just wait . . . soon missionaries will no longer be welcome!"

Climbing the hill hand in hand that day they discussed what this would mean to Christianity in India. It was a great temptation to dismiss the idea as something that couldn't happen.

"India will need *new* missionaries to replace the old ones," Paul suggested thoughtfully. "Indians, instead of foreigners, who are willing to take the Gospel to their own people in every village."

"They will need training!" said Devi earnestly.

"That will be the great problem," Paul sighed. He walked beside her in silence, lost in thought for some time. At last he spoke, and there was a sadness that she had not heard before in his voice. "God has blessed my ministry. But of the converts I have won to Christ, how many are preaching the Gospel? That question shames me, because I know the sad answer."

"It isn't your fault. Perhaps God has not called them to be preachers."

"None of them . . . ?"

They reached the top of the hill and stood together watching the clouds moving in from the coast. Suddenly Paul turned to Devi, an intense, almost fierce look in his eyes. "God is saying something to me that I find hard to understand . . . that I must start a Bible school where our own people can be trained to win India for Christ!"

They prayed together about it that day, but the idea seemed too preposterous, embarrassingly visionary and impractical. Paul mentioned it no more while in Mercara. But he could not shake this conviction, and it began to trouble him increasingly.

It was a sad but exciting day when they left Mercara by bus for the railway center of Mysore. Still uncertain about where God was leading them, they had promised to spend a few days with Devi's parents in Narsapur, 500 miles to the northeast on the Bay of Bengal. It would have been unthinkable to discuss their finances with her husband: therefore Devi wasn't aware that Paul had only some small change left after buying tickets on the night train to Bangalore—which was still 350 miles short of Narsapur!

Sitting beside Paul, Devi slept fitfully, awakened by every station stop—wondering, half afraid, whether this long train ride was just a sample of the nomadic life they would live together. With the first rays of dawn, sleep left her completely, and renewed anxieties occupied her mind as she disinterestedly watched the monsoon-drenched landscape slip monotonously past. Paul offered little conversation, seeming to be deep in thought, praying silently she supposed. He made no move to buy food when the train stopped now and then at a town. As the morning wore on, Devi became increasingly hungry, but said nothing. It was not her place to express her feelings. Her husband must know her needs and meet them. She still held him in awe. He was a man, and she had been sheltered from men all of her life. Living with one day and night was still a strange experience.

It was midmorning when at last they reached Bangalore. Carrying their bags off the train, Paul led the way into the half-filled waiting room, praying inwardly for the Lord to show him what to do.

"What can I get you for breakfast?" he asked Devi when they had seated themselves wearily beside their baggage.

"Just for *me?*" Devi sensed that something was wrong. Had she offended him? She tried to think back over the morning, the night before.

"Devi . . . ," Paul began hesitantly. He would have to tell her the truth. "I didn't want you to worry, so I said nothing, but our tickets don't go any farther, and I have no money . . . just enough to buy your breakfast." Now it was out. He looked at her with sympathy. Her lip was trembling.

"No more money?" she asked weakly, twisting the loose end of her sari nervously, unbelief and shock in her eyes. "None at all?"

"That's not unusual," said Paul gently, "but the Lord always provides." He put his hand gently on her shoulder, but she turned away.

Her body was shaking with suppressed sobs. This was what she had feared! "If only you had told me! I could have written to my father for money! Now how will we get to Narsapur . . . or anywhere?" The words poured out of her like water through a broken dam. She was crying audibly now, trying not to.

"It would bankrupt your father to support us—and we don't need him!" replied Paul. "My heavenly Father has *never* failed. . . ."

"Perhaps if you held some meetings in town . . . ," said Devi uncertainly, daubing at her tears. "But what can God do in a train station?"

"Let us see!" said Paul with characteristic simplicity reflecting the confidence in God he had learned and lived. "We'll ask him!" Kneeling down beside the bench he motioned to Devi to kneel with him. "Lord, you know what our needs are," he began in a loud voice. "We're trusting in the living God. . . ." On he prayed, oblivious to the curious stares.

An army captain in uniform was looking at Paul as though he couldn't believe his eyes, and stepped forward, hand extended, smiling broadly, the moment Paul stood to his feet. "Brother Gupta!" he exclaimed warmly. "I didn't expect to see *you* here! What a pleasant surprise! And this must be your wife!"

"Yes," replied Paul hesitantly. The voice sounded familiar, but he couldn't place the face. Then he remembered. Of course! Dr. Kotalinga! "I've never seen you in uniform!" he exclaimed. "No wonder I didn't recognize you." Turning to Devi he said, "This is Dr. Kotalinga. I've stayed in his home often in Secunderabad."

"My wife will be delighted. . . ." said the captain. Hurrying out onto the platform, he returned with a stout but handsome woman in a bright sari, trying to keep up with his long strides.

"I'm so happy to meet you!" exclaimed Mrs. Kotalinga to Devi. "My husband and I wanted so much to come to your wedding . . . but we're both military doctors, and our schedule wouldn't allow it. How wonderful to find you here! We just came to meet some officers. That's their train arriving now."

Losing some of her shyness, Devi was smiling, warmed by the enthusiastic friendliness of this pair. "I'm very glad to meet you," she replied. "My husband has told me about you. You've been very kind to him."

"I'm sorry we have to rush off." Fumbling through her handbag Mrs. Kotalinga pulled out an envelope. "I've been carrying this around for weeks not knowing where to mail it." She handed it to Devi. "It's our wedding gift, dear. I'm so sorry we couldn't have been there."

"Oh, thank you!" said Devi, taking the envelope gratefully.

With a quick farewell the Kotalingas hurried back onto the platform, leaving Paul and Devi looking at each other in open-mouthed wonder as though they had just been visited by two angels.

With trembling fingers Devi tore open the envelope. "Look! Money! Lots of it!"

"Thank you, Lord, for answering our prayer," Paul said quietly, holding Devi's hand in his. "Help us always to trust you!" After buying tickets for the rest of the trip to Narsapur, enough money was left to live on for a week.

In the stack of mail awaiting them was a letter begging Paul to return to Kharagpur in West Bengal, where he had already preached a number of times. The pastor of the Baptist church there did not accept the basic teachings of Scripture. Tiring of sermons that were more social than biblical, part of the congregation, including several American servicemen stationed at the large U.S. air base nearby, had started to meet for worship in homes. They needed someone to shepherd them. After praying, Paul and Devi were both convinced that God was telling them to respond to this call for help.

Preaching and teaching during the following months in Kharagpur, Paul baptized about sixty new believers. Some of them came to Christ in remarkable ways. Early one morning, while in prayer, Paul felt an urgent desire to visit the headmaster of the local school. Fearful that Mr. Kidd, no doubt still in bed, would be angry at being disturbed at such an early hour, Paul nevertheless bicycled obediently to his home and knocked on the door, confident that the Lord had sent him.

After a long delay, Mr. Kidd, still in his pajamas, opened the door. "Paul Gupta!" he exclaimed, surprised but obviously glad to see him. "Please come in! God has sent you!"

In a distraught voice he told Paul that because of a quarrel his wife had just left him, taking the children with her. Despondent, he had been preparing to commit suicide when the knock had come at his door. Now he knew that God loved him, because he had sent Paul just in time. After Paul explained the Gospel to him once again, they knelt together in prayer, and Mr. Kidd received Christ into his heart as his Savior and Lord. Soon afterward his wife also became a believer and the family was reunited. Paul had the joy of baptizing husband and wife together.

Not long after arriving in Kharagpur, Devi's faith was tested again. One morning their food supply ran out completely. That night they went to bed with empty stomachs. Paul left early the next morning on his bicycle to make his rounds of visiting converts, preaching in the streets, and Bible teaching for women who would gather in various homes. Alone in their small rented room, Devi was praying, reminding herself of God's faithfulness at the train station in Bangalore, yet fearful that she would have nothing for Paul's supper.

Early in the afternoon there was a knock on the door. It was Dr. Simon, a medical doctor living on the other side of town. His arms were filled with groceries: rice, meat, vegetables.

"The Lord burdened my heart to bring this to you," he said, adding apologetically, "I don't know whether you need it or not."

"Need it, brother?" exclaimed Devi gratefully. "God has sent you! We have nothing!"

Paul's heart was heavily burdened as he pedaled his bicycle home that evening. How could he tell Devi that the Lord had not provided any money for food and they must go hungry again tonight? He was concerned that she not become discouraged with this life of faith. He opened the door slowly, rehearsing some words of encouragement, and was met by the miraculous aroma of goat curry cooking! Dr. Simon arrived later to share the meal, and together they rejoiced in God's love. This was the way they were to live, and Devi began to enjoy this dependence upon God for everything that made his presence and care so much more real than she had known before.

Not many months later Paul and Devi were able to help Dr. Simon. After rescuing a Moslem woman from a mob of Hindus bent on murdering her, then rescuing a Hindu man from a Moslem mob, this godly doctor had to flee for his life. Paul and Devi took him in where they were staying, with a family Paul had led to Christ. The fabled Independence had not yet come, but already the riots had started that would give the full lie to Hinduism's two main tenets: nonviolence and the unity of all religions. That there was no unity between Hinduism and Islam, and no tolerance by either for the other would be fully demonstrated to the world. One of the great costs of Independence would be the partition of India into two separate countries on religious grounds: Pakistan for Moslems and India for Hindus. The latter would be as much to blame as the former for partition, showing little willingness to assure the Moslem minority of fair treatment, and virtually forcing them to fight for their own separate country.

Mohammed Ali Jinnah, the iron-willed leader of India's Moslems, had vowed, "We shall have India divided or we shall have India destroyed." The Moslem League declared August 16, 1946, "Direct Action Day"—a demonstration to Britain and the Hindu majority that Jinnah spoke the truth. Screaming for Hindu blood, Moslem mobs swarmed out of Calcutta's "worst slums on earth" and beat to death every Hindu in their path, while the police fled for their lives. Such "action" was hardly surprising, since Islam's converts by the millions had been convinced at the point of a sword, and the Koran offered heaven for killing heathen. But the Hindus, their doctrine of ahimsa notwithstanding, were no less violent. Hindu mobs roamed Calcutta slaughtering Moslems in revenge. The toll in the first twenty-four hours was more than 6,000 dead.

Murderous riots broke out all over India. Howling mobs ruled the streets of Kharagpur for a time. Making his rounds by bicycle, Paul saw mutilated bodies beside the road and sometimes in front of homes where entire families had been pulled out of a house and murdered simply because they belonged to another religion. This was happening in India, where sages and gurus proclaimed all religions to be one. Gandhi worked tirelessly and heroically, at times going on foot from burned-out village to burned-out village, preaching brotherhood and tolerance, but to no avail. His reward would be death by an assassin's bullet, and his killer a fellow Hindu at that.

The worst bloodshed followed immediately after Independence in August 1947. Pursued by murderous mobs, about five million Hindus escaped from Pakistan into India, while an equal number of Moslems fled in the opposite direction, many to be ambushed and slaughtered just before reaching safety. At least 100,000, and probably far more, died horrible deaths at the hands of Hindu and Moslem mobs in one of the greatest orgies of bloodshed and cruelty the world has ever known. What a spectacle to see Hindus, who would not swat a mosquito or eat meat in order not to take life, beating Moslems to a bloody pulp with a ferocity and hatred that were beyond description!

So much for nonviolence and the unity of all religions. Hindus themselves had fully shown that these theories did not fit the facts of human existence, yet strangely enough their faith in Hinduism remained unshaken. All of Gandhi's efforts to teach his countrymen to practice the love and brotherhood they professed were ultimately of no avail, in spite of momentary successes along the way. Something more was needed—a solution of another kind. If Paul and Devi had wanted any further proof that Christ is the only hope for this world, they needed it no more. Nor could Paul any longer doubt that he was to start a school for training Indians to preach the Gospel of Christ all over India.

It was obvious, however, that he must first attend a Bible college. How could he train others without being trained himself? But having investigated the Bible colleges in India he had not been able to find one of sound evangelical doctrine: all denied to some extent the inspiration of Scripture and the cardinal tenets of Christian faith. He would have to go to England or America for training. Friends he discussed this vision with were all against it—Bakt Singh, Silas Fox, Dr. Raju, the Christians in Kharagpur—and most thought it was madness even to imagine going back to school, much less starting one. Surely if God wanted an evangelical Bible school in India he would have given that vision to someone who was already qualified. Now that Devi had seen how effectively God was using Paul in many lives, she too thought it would be a mistake to give up a ministry that was so successful.

But another and more pressing consideration had entered their thinking: Devi was pregnant and the baby would have to be given top priority in any future plans. "I have to take care of my baby," became Devi's standard objection. "I couldn't go with you."

Paul agreed. The baby's arrival would change everything. How could he leave Devi alone with an infant? And it was out of the question to think of all three of them going to England or America

—not just the inconvenience and difficulties but the cost would be prohibitive. And why should he quit preaching in the streets and churches of India when God was saving so many souls through his efforts? He enjoyed doing what he was doing and didn't want to go back to school. The baby was a convenient excuse. Indeed, it had become more important than anything else to Paul and Devi even before it was born.

In the seventh month of her pregnancy, Devi, as was customary, went to stay with her parents, who could hardly wait for the birth of the child. How good God was to bless them in this way. Some of the harsh things relatives had said about Paul and the bleak predictions that had been made for this marriage were being retracted now. The arrival of a son, whom everyone expected to be named Paul, would change all of that.

The excitement bursting inside Paul could hardly be suppressed when he arrived at the Raju home at the last moment from Kharagpur. One of his wife's uncles met him at the door with a broad smile. "You're just in time!" he exclaimed. "She's been in labor since four this morning."

The house was filled with excited relatives who had come from far and near for this big event. When Paul joined them in the front room they all stood up to greet him enthusiastically, offering congratulations. It was a happy group, full of talk about the size and sex of the baby—with most people sure it would be a boy because Devi had looked so large and of course everyone knows that boy babies are larger than girls. Those with children of their own enumerated for Paul the joys of parenthood, and also some of its responsibilities and problems. Everyone had plenty of advice . . . and so the time passed as they all waited happily with suppressed excitement.

The baby was not coming easily for Devi. She had been in labor for nearly eighteen hours and was semianesthetized by exhaustion. The mission hospital, as usual, had closed for the summer. The staff had fled to the mountains from the unbearable heat and humidity, after sending the patients home with enough medications to last until missionary doctors and nurses returned with the cooling monsoon rains. So Devi was having the baby at home rather than going to the nearest government hospital in another town. After all, her father was a medical doctor, and so was a Christian aunt who came to assist in the birth. A registered nurse and a midwife completed the impressive medical staff on hand in the sickroom.

At last, with one final surging intensity of pain, the baby was delivered into Dr. Raju's eager hands. After losing consciousness briefly, Devi opened her eyes to see her father holding up a handsome boy with wisps of curly black hair on his head, and bright eyes that seemed to dart everywhere in surprise.

"He's a large one—almost twelve pounds—and *perfect!*" exclaimed Dr. Raju with the ill-concealed pride of a grandfather.

What a beautiful gift from God! The baby was strong, lifting and turning his head, trying to peer inquisitively all around the room. Devi thought he even smiled at her—then her eyes closed in fatigue. A tiny round face danced before her. She could see it so plainly, that half smile on its lips, the brightness of its eyes, those wisps of fine hair already formed. Her first baby, a son for Paul, not crying or fussing, looking so alert. A handsome boy, and such a strong and healthy one! There would be no more criticism of Paul now! Everybody would have to admit that he was a good husband who had cared well for her. And they would have to admit also that God's blessing was on their marriage. Their heavenly Father had given them a son.

"My little baby, I will take good care of you!" she whispererd as she drifted contentedly into the surrealistic world of dreams.

Suddenly Dr. Raju stiffened. The baby had stopped breathing! He turned it over and hit it on the back. Putting it down on a table he worked feverishly, with the help of the other doctor, to revive it, but there was not a flutter of the eyelids, not another beat of the heart. It was gone! And for all of his medical knowledge, Dr. Raju had no explanation. It was one of those freak happenings that remain forever a mystery . . . unless one believes in God.

9

"I Serve a Remarkable God"

The tragic news, announced in solemn voice by Devi's aunt, sent a wave of shock through the crowded room where the relatives were waiting in happy expectation. Burying his face in his hands, Paul began to weep quietly. It couldn't be true! The Lord had been so good to them. How could he have allowed this to happen?

Hindu relatives present began to wail inconsolably, for there is no hope and no comfort in Hinduism. What good to believe loved ones have been reincarnated if one will never see them again? And when all have reached their final destination of absorption into the Absolute, what will remain of the love once experienced together? Paul knew that he would one day see his child alive in the presence of the King of kings; nevertheless it wasn't easy to bear such a heavy loss. Harder still to understand why it had happened. There were others in the room, however, for whom this was no mystery.

"It's because she married a man that goes about the streets preaching. They have no proper home. He doesn't take care of her, so of course the baby couldn't be healthy. See what comes of giving your daughter to a man who has neither property nor job. . . ."

Paul was rescued momentarily from the agony of overhearing these callous remarks when his father-in-law appeared in the doorway motioning for him. "You can stay just a few moments," Dr. Raju whispered as they made their way to the back of the house. "She doesn't know the child is dead—we put it in the bed next to her as though it's asleep. Don't look so sad—she mustn't know until she's had some rest."

"Did you see him?" Devi asked weakly when Paul bent over and kissed her.

He nodded and squeezed her hand, too choked to speak.

Her large eyes looked up into his. "Isn't he beautiful?" There was a mother's pride in her voice, asking for approval.

"He's a handsome baby," Paul agreed. Dr. Raju was pulling at his arm. "You need to sleep now," he said, kissing her again. Taking one more look at the dead baby, he walked from the room with drooping shoulders and bent head. Why? Why?

Awakened the next morning by the first rays of dawn, Devi struggled to sit up, calling for her baby. The nurse gently pushed her back onto the pillow. "He's still asleep," she said.

An hour later Devi was wide awake again, looking at the baby, demanding to hold him. The truth could no longer be hidden. With halting words punctuated by brave efforts to hold back the tears, her mother told her how the baby had suddenly and mysteriously died. "The Lord has given, and the Lord has taken away," she said. "The ways of God are not our ways. We must accept his will."

Devi would not, or could not, believe it. She began to sob hysterically, demanding to have her baby, trying to get out of bed. There was no way to calm her but to let her have the tiny corpse. She cuddled it, insisting it was only asleep and would awaken soon for feeding. Afraid that she was losing her mind, her father and aunt finally persuaded her that the dead must be buried. When Devi at last let go of her firstborn, she began to cry piteously, and there was no comforting her.

It was Sunday and Paul had been scheduled to preach at Bethany Gospel Chapel, where they had been married little more than a year before. Most of the congregation had been guests at the wedding, and a turmoil of memories swept over him when he stood up to face them; but by God's grace he was able to preach of Christ's love without breaking down in tears. Afterward there was a brief funeral service in the Raju home attended by close friends and relatives; then the tiny, lifeless form lying in the hastily prepared wooden casket was taken by bullock cart and buried in the Christian cemetery on the other side of town. The finality of seeing the small grave filled with dirt broke Paul down. He stood beside the mound of fresh earth crying, "Why? Why?"

When the others had left for the cemetery, Devi cried herself to sleep. It was early afternoon when she awakened. Outside she could hear udutha, the tiny squirrel with chipmunk stripes, screaming in its high voice. How often as a girl she had watched its antics on the rooftop, as it taunted the crows until one of them dove at it—then with a lightning flick of its tail in the clumsy bird's face, the impish creature would dash down the gable, scolding saucily. The smells and sounds coming through the window made her head throb with child-hood memories: playing with the dolls she and her cousins used to make out of paper and tie with bright ribbons, playing wedding day and dreaming of the time when she would be married, and, happiest day of all, would present her parents with a grandson. There was no sweetness now in such remembrances—only bitterness and deep pain. Deeper still was the voice that echoed in her conscience: "You have said, '*I* must care for *my* baby, I can't go to Bible school because of *my* baby. *My* baby, *my* baby, *my* baby.' Now you will see that it is *My* baby, and *I* will take care of it!"

"God has been speaking loudly to my heart," Paul said to Devi when he returned from preaching again that evening. "We have put the baby first. I have been disobedient, refusing to obey God's will. I didn't want the responsibility of starting a Bible school—but now I'm willing, even to go far away for training."

Devi began to cry. "It's my fault," she said between sobs. "I have said, '*My* baby, *my* baby.' Because of that the Lord had to show us that we have nothing to call our own. We belong to him, and so does the baby. He has taken it away in judgment. I'm sorry!" She wept bitterly, while Paul waited, tears running down his own cheeks. At last she said, "Whatever he wants me to do, wherever he wants me to go, I'll obey gladly."

Having made that surrender did not remove the grief for Devi. She had looked forward to this event for so long, confident that the baby's birth would remove the reproach she had felt so keenly and suffered in silence since her marriage. Instead, the death of the child had poured fresh fuel on the flames of gossip. She could hear the tormenting words drifting to her through the open door from other rooms in the house. Worse still, friends and relatives who came in to visit told her to her face.

"This man hasn't cared for you," they would say. "He has given you no proper home, you've had so many worries because of wondering where the next meal would come from. . . ."

"It isn't true!" Devi would break in fervently. "Paul is a good husband. He always cared for me. God has provided for all of our needs—but we made the baby an excuse for avoiding what God wanted us to do, so our heavenly Father took it away."

That explanation only gave another reason for criticism. Who could believe that God was calling Paul Gupta to start a Bible college? He hadn't completed high school himself! Where would it be? Who would want to attend it? And the money to pay for this lunatic's dream—where would *that* come from? The sooner Devi got Paul to forget that wild fantasy, the better. They would come to complete disaster launching out on this fool's errand!

Devi had developed severe complications, and the medical opinion was that she could never have another child. Paul rejected this prognosis with characteristic contempt for what he called "man's opinions," vowing that he would listen only to God.

Back in Kharagpur, Paul and Devi prayed earnestly about the future. It was a burden they had to bear alone. Everyone else was against the idea of Paul's going away to school and eventually starting a Bible college. "This is not God's will for you!" Bakt Singh had bluntly told him. That would have been enough to shake almost anyone's faith, since Bakt Singh was regarded as an apostle and thousands sought his blessing with the laying on of hands and accepted whatever he said as a word from the Lord. But Paul had not been swayed. "I have not asked for your guidance!" he had courageously replied. "I'm following the Lord—not man!" Nor had he been swayed by Silas Fox's caustic comment that "seminaries are cemeteries," in his attempt to discourage him. The Christians in Kharagpur were now Paul's closest friends, but they offered him no support in what they called this "wild scheme." Nevertheless, Paul and Devi remained confident that they had not misunderstood God's will.

It was not enough just to pray. Paul was a man of action, having long ago learned that one must do all he could, and only then would God do his part. The first step of faith was to get passports for both of them. Ordinarily this would have been a lengthy and even costly affair—but God had given Paul a Christian friend in Calcutta, who put his official signature as a magistrate on the application, opening the way to get the passports in two hours instead of several weeks. He also wrote a letter of guarantee for 20,000 rupees, required of all Indian citizens wishing to leave the country. Paul and Devi accepted this "parting of the Red Sea" as a further sign that they were in God's will.

As his next step of faith, Paul applied to London Bible College and was accepted—but so far he didn't have a rupee for passage or tuition. Praying about that, Paul thought of an American serviceman, Harold Farmer, who had been stationed during the war at the huge airbase near Kharagpur, used for bombing along the Burma Road and into China. Harold had attended some of Paul's meetings, and Paul remembered that he was now a student at Moody Bible Institute. Perhaps that was the school to attend. No one in Kharagpur could locate Harold's address: but a friend gave Paul the address of Bill Wood, another former American serviceman, who had also attended meetings in Kharagpur and was now living in Los Angeles. Paul wrote a letter to Harold Farmer in care of Bill Wood, whom he had never met, expecting him to forward it. Thinking the letter was to him, Bill opened it by mistake. But there are no mistakes with God —and that simple act changed the course of Paul's life. Noting that

Paul was asking Harold about Moody Bible Institute, Bill immediately sent him application forms for the Bible Institute of Los Angeles, and encouraged him to apply there.

M.B.I. informed Paul that first-year students were not allowed to work. He must have his full tuition and costs in hand for the first year before he could be accepted. Biola, however, not only accepted Paul enthusiastically, but the dean promised that the school would provide him with a part-time job that would pay enough for his tuition and expenses. Here was a mountain removed! When the American Consul in Madras issued a visa on the strength of the dean's letter, Paul and Devi took that as a sign from the Lord to attend Biola. Although Paul didn't have a rupee toward his fare, he began confidently to tell friends that he would be leaving for Los Angeles in time to start the spring semester at Biola. His friends smiled patronizingly, certain that it couldn't happen.

On the first day of September 1948, after very brief labor, Devi gave birth to a healthy, handsome baby boy. They named him Johnny. The doctors were amazed, but there he was, a gift from the Lord! The death of her first child had resulted in a change of policy for the mission hospital, which never closed down for the summer again, causing Devi to hope that the laying down of that one life might save many in the future. Even more important, she was confident that the sacrifice of that life would yet result in eternal salvation for many through the training of new missionaries to spread the Gospel all over India.

About a month after Johnny's birth Paul took another step of faith —one that seemed foolhardy to the few friends he confided in. He sold his bicycle, so vital for his ministry in India, and used that money, a mere 75 rupees, for a deposit to hold reservations on a freighter—the cheapest way to go—leaving Calcutta for Boston in little more than two months. The balance he needed was 2,500 rupees, a sum that wouldn't have seemed more impossible if it had been 25,000.

As the weeks went by, a few small gifts began to come in, but they were like a drop in the ocean. "Are you still leaving on that ship in January?" friends would ask skeptically. "By God's grace I'm going!" Paul would reply. During this time he read again the lives of men like George Mueller and C. T. Studd. Their testimonies helped strengthen his own confidence in the Lord. "I serve the same God they served," Paul would say, "and he will do the same miracles for me that he did for them." His father-in-law considered that the height of presumption. "They were from a Christian country," he told Paul, "where there were thousands of believers to support them. But where will *your* support come from in this Hindu land?" Paul's faith was very simple. "It will come from the Lord!" he replied without hesitation.

In early December, just a month before sailing, a check for 1,000 rupees, more money than Paul had ever held in his hands, arrived along with a letter of encouragement from Harold Farmer in Chicago. "The Lord is faithful!" Paul exclaimed. "This is the beginning!" Preaching at the annual conference at Bethany Gospel Chapel in Narsapur, standing before that crowd of more than 5,000 people, he announced that he was leaving for America and bade them all goodbye.

Two days before the ship was to sail, Paul arrived in Calcutta with exactly 2,500 rupees in his pocket, the last of it having come from the sale of Devi's jewelry, a cherished possession for every Indian woman, representing her life's savings held for emergency. Testing their faith, the Lord had waited until the last moment to provide the necessary funds. Paul had left for Calcutta still 100 rupees short, and that had been given to him by someone he met on the train.

The friend Paul stayed with his last night in India played a trick on him that he would never forget. After dinner as they were talking about Paul's departure for America, his host casually said, "Let's see what's on the news." Reaching over he turned on the radio.

"Special bulletin!" said an excited voice. Paul leaned forward with concern. Had new riots erupted here in Calcutta? "A desperate communist agent sought by the police, alias Paul Gupta, real name Nagaruru Vankateswami Gupta, was reportedly seen today in Calcutta. It is suspected that he is about to flee by ship to the United States. The docks are being closely watched. There is a 5,000-rupee reward for information leading to his arrest. Approach with caution —he is probably armed and considered to be extremely dangerous."

Thoroughly taken in by the "broadcast," Paul couldn't understand how such a mistake could have been made. "I have nothing to hide," he said very seriously. "I'm not a communist, and you know that I'm not dangerous except to the enemies of Christ."

"Oh, it's just a trick," said his host, unable to keep a straight face any longer. "See here." He showed Paul and his family a recorder connected to the radio and explained that he had faked the broadcast. Everyone had a good laugh.

Paul was not laughing the next day when he stood at the counter facing the steamship agent and heard him adamantly refuse to sell him the ticket to Boston.

"But I have the full price!" Paul protested, waving the money at him. "This ticket has been reserved for me for two months!"

"You're not listening to me," came the icily polite reply. "All passengers entering the United States must carry a minimum of $50 in traveler's checks—which you don't have."

"But no one told me about that! Why is this $50 required?"

"To be sure visitors to America have some spending money and won't be begging in the streets."

"I don't need spending money," said Paul earnestly. "God is my banker. He takes care of me."

The ticket agent looked at Paul as though he were insane. "God may be your banker," he scoffed, "but without that $50 you're not getting a ticket!"

Turning away in bewilderment, Paul stared out the window over the rooftops of Calcutta, seeing nothing. "Lord, I don't know what you're trying to teach me now," he prayed quietly, "but I know you brought me this far. Please get me on that ship!"

Opening his eyes, Paul saw a messenger delivering a telegram. The ticket agent opened it casually. As he read, his eyes grew wide with astonishment and his face paled with apparent shock.

Turning to Paul he exclaimed, "You're a remarkable man! This telegram is from American Express in New York ordering me to give you $50 in traveler's checks!"

"Thank you, Lord!" Paul said aloud. "Thank you, Lord!"

"You are a *remarkable* man!" the ticket agent repeated in awe.

"*I* am not remarkable," Paul replied happily, "but I serve a remarkable God!"

10

In the Heavenly Father's Care

Except for the howling North Atlantic storm, the trip to Boston was relatively uneventful. The twelve passengers aboard the British freighter ate with the officers, and at each meal Paul talked enthusiastically about Christ. When the chief engineer one day burst out with, "I'm sick and tired of this religious stuff all the time!" Paul was shocked. Apparently all westerners were not Christians after all—and he had thought they were!

From Boston he traveled to Chicago by bus. There he was met at the Greyhound depot by Harold Farmer, the M.B.I. student who had sent him the 1,000 rupees that had paid for nearly half of his fare to America. "It's good to see you, Paul!" Harold greeted him when he climbed wearily off the bus after the all-night ride.

"And I'm glad to see you, brother!" Paul exclaimed in relief. It was confusing to travel alone in this strange land, where people spoke American instead of English, and there were no meandering cows, snail-paced bullock carts, and streams of bicycles clogging the roads, no one sleeping on the sidewalk—but everyone seemed in such a frightful hurry, madly dashing about in huge cars, the women wearing such scandalously short skirts, and none of the men wearing dhotis, only pants. And people seemed as tall as giants. In a land like this, having friends to meet one along the way was a real blessing!

As Harold drove through Chicago traffic toward the Institute, he inquired about the believers in Kharagpur, and listened with joy as Paul told about the many like Mr. and Mrs. Kidd who had accepted

Christ and been baptized. Suddenly Harold seemed to remember something important. "Say . . . I wanted to ask you, did you get that $50 I sent at the last moment?"

"You sent it?" Paul exclaimed.

"Yes. So you got it?"

"I wondered who sent it! Brother, let me tell you, it was a miracle the way that arrived just in time. I couldn't have gotten on the ship without it! How did you happen to send it just then?"

"I felt so strongly that you needed another $50," replied Harold, "but I'm on the GI Bill—that's a government program for students that barely provides our expenses—and I had no money. When my next check came I was afraid it was too late, but it seemed so urgent that I had traveler's checks cabled to you at the last place I thought you could be reached, the ticket office in Calcutta."

"Praise God!" Paul exclaimed gratefully. "That money arrived at the very time I was in that office. But it's even more miraculous. The first stop that ship made after leaving Calcutta was Madras. Had I known that I wouldn't have gone to Calcutta!"

"I didn't realize that either," said Harold soberly. "How marvelously God works! But you still need $100 registration fee."

"We'll trust the Lord for that, too," came the quick reply.

By the time he boarded the train for Los Angeles, Paul had formed many new and lasting friendships in Chicago: and from church offerings and individual gifts he had received exactly the $100 he needed for registration at Biola.

To be actually studying in Los Angeles at a Bible Institute seemed almost unreal—or was that long-ago and faraway life as a Hindu just a dream? Often as Paul looked back on his life it was hard to fit the pieces together. Devout Hindu named after a god . . . failure at high school . . . debauchery and stealing from his own father . . . and now studying at the Bible Institute of Los Angeles, preparing to open a Bible institute in India! Yet the God who had created him and who had sent that missionary right to the front of his house to preach about "salvation for *sinners*" had known it all for an eternity. He also knew the future, and Paul was happy to be in his hands.

That first semester passed quickly in long hours of study and lots of preaching all over southern California in churches of many denominations and on various radio programs. Paul never learned what the part-time job Biola had promised really was, because he was kept too busy preaching to do any other work, and the offerings he received were enough to pay his way. And if that hadn't been enough, Bill Wood had met him at the train station when he had arrived in Los Angeles with the promise to take care of his needs that first semester. God was so good!

Everywhere he went people were fascinated to hear how a high-caste Hindu had become a follower of Christ: but Paul was a preacher, not just a story teller. The audiences he spoke to were deeply moved and challenged, and many were the tears of repentance that were shed as people came forward in his meetings to receive Christ or to rededicate themselves to Him.

Kipling had said, "East is East, and West is West, and never the twain shall meet . . ." but Paul was discovering that people are the same everywhere. In America the churches were also full of nominal Christians—and, as in India, "converts" could become a great disappointment. He was particularly touched by the sad story told to him by one of many who came forward when he preached at the Union Rescue Mission. "You can't get a good job with those old clothes you're wearing," Paul told him. Taking the new convert to his room, Paul dressed him in his own blue wedding suit, optimistic that he would now find a job and be able to lead a new life. Paul's joy turned to sorrow, and the hurt that comes from being deceived, when later he learned that the blue wedding suit had been promptly sold to buy more booze. Another reminder that although God is willing, man must be willing also.

With his warm smile and outgoing, positive personality, Paul made many lasting friendships. In his irrepressible way, exuding a childlike, uncomplicated faith, he let everyone know that he was studying in

America because God wanted him to start a Bible school in India for training Indians to evangelize their own country. It never occurred to Paul to worry about the odds against such a dream ever being fulfilled. That was God's problem, and he could do anything. Some people thought he was a naïve enthusiast. Others were inspired with a new vision and began to pray for this faroff land and its multiplying millions.

That first Sunday in Los Angeles, standing in front of the Church of the Open Door, adjoining Biola in those days, Paul met a young man named Ed Murphy. They became close friends. Ed had been raised a strict Roman Catholic, and explained to Paul how his church membership and the rituals he participated in had actually hindered his spiritual quest by keeping him so busy "serving" God and trying to appease him that he had been unable to see that Christ's death and Resurrection made it possible for him to be forgiven and to receive as a free gift the salvation he had tried for years to merit by religious observances. Trusting in his relationship to the church, he had missed a personal relationship with Christ. Paul began to see that Catholic or Protestant religiosity was very similar to Hinduism. East and West were very much alike after all. The images and rituals were different, but the underlying error was the same: deceiving the followers of all religions with the lie that repeated prayers and ritual, personal effort and sacrifice would appease God and elevate the worshiper into fellowship or oneness with him.

Ed was fascinated to discover that Paul, raised an idol worshiper, knew the Bible far better and walked more intimately with Christ than he, who had been raised in "Christian" America. Paul began to disciple Ed as Silas Fox had discipled him, passing on the many lessons he had learned from men like Pastor Joseph, the godly headmaster, Mr. Daniel in Madras, Agrippa, Bakt Singh: a passion for lost souls, the life of prayer and faith, walking in the Spirit, and how effectively to preach the Gospel. Ed would learn more about living the Christian life from this converted Hindu than from all his Bible Institute courses. He looked upon Paul as a missionary from India to America.

Sometimes when they traveled together Ed would be awakened from a deep sleep in the middle of the night by the sound of muffled sobs, and, peering through the darkness, he would see Paul on his knees crying to God for lost souls and for the enduement with the power of the Holy Spirit in order to reach them with the Gospel.

Paul had planned to attend summer school in order to finish his studies sooner, but God had planned otherwise. A fellow student named Clyde Daly offered to drive Paul on a preaching tour across the country during summer vacation. It was one of those foolish ideas —two young men with no contacts in a country where pastors jealously guard pulpits and offerings, setting out in a thirteen-year-old Dodge—that God loves to bless with his miracles to his glory. Clyde had heard Paul preach only once, at a large sheriff's detention center north of Los Angeles, and had been much impressed by the large number of young men who had gone forward to receive Christ.

Having no real plans, Clyde drove first to Bend, Oregon, where a stepbrother lived. In this unlikely region of scattered small towns on the dry desert east of the beautiful Cascade mountains, Paul held twenty meetings. Night after night as he preached, God's Spirit spoke powerfully and many came forward with tears of repentance. These lives, touched by an ex-Hindu, would never be the same again. Many of the friendships made among those simple country folk would endure a lifetime. Before leaving eastern Oregon's seemingly inhospitable plain, Paul had been given enough money to bring his wife and baby son to join him in Los Angeles. It seemed a miracle! When he had said that tearful good-bye to Devi, they had not expected to see one another for five years. Now after only seven months, as an unexpected gift from his heavenly Father, he had the money for plane tickets, and all she needed was a guarantor. Surely the Lord knew how that need would also be supplied.

Passing through the Chicago area a few weeks later, Paul stopped to see Dr. John Rice. "What about your wife, brother?" Dr. Rice asked. "When do you think you'll be able to bring her to the States?"

"The Lord has wonderfully supplied her air fare," Paul replied, "but she can't get a visa until she has a guarantor."

"You mean someone to guarantee her support in this country?"

"Yes. Please remember to pray about that."

"I don't pray about anything I can do myself," came the blunt but loving reply. "I'll give you the letter of guarantee!"

Back at Biola for the fall semester, Clyde and Paul found their fellow students excited to hear how God had guided them on their summer tour. No one, however, was half as excited as Paul. God had used him, a former Hindu, to change and challenge many lives in wealthy, sophisticated America. Proof enough that God could use native Indians to evangelize India! The foreign missionaries, all white men, often gave the impression that Indian believers were incapable of Christian leadership. Many Indian Christians felt this inferiority keenly after living under British rule all their lives. It had been his fellow Indians who had told him he was dreaming an impossible dream. But now God had strengthened his faith. If in God's hands he could be an effective missionary to the United States—and during the summer many people had called him that—then surely Indian Christians could be effective missionaries in their own land. And when Paul thought of the expense of traveling from a foreign country that would be saved, and the difficult adjustments that would be eliminated for a strange climate, culture, and language, he rejoiced at the divine wisdom that was guiding him.

With Devi and Johnny soon to arrive, Paul began to look for an apartment. It would have to be a cheap one, and close to Biola. Eventually he found one, north of the downtown library, in an old, run-down tenement district destined to be demolished for a freeway. Not the most savory neighborhood, with its chronic alcoholics and prostitutes: but to a man still inexperienced in American ways, it was the best he could find at the price, and it certainly looked like paradise compared to the ramshackle slums of India, fashioned from mud, palm branches, scrap metal, packing crates, and whatever—so Paul didn't know that he had moved to the slums of Los Angeles. Friends helped him clean and paint.

The first phone call he had after moving in was from a friend he had met at Villa Chapel, a small Brethren Assembly in Pasadena. "Some of us would like to come over and visit you, Paul," she said.

"Maybe later . . . ," he began, groping for an excuse. Their homes were so beautiful—but *this*. . . . "I don't even have a chair for you to sit on yet." It was embarrassing.

"That's what I'm calling about—we want to help." And they did! Mrs. Ertl, Mrs. Granley, Miss LeTourneaux, and others brought in beds, tables, chairs—even dishes, linens, and everything else Devi would need to set up housekeeping when she arrived. It wasn't Beverly Hills, but at least now it was comfortable, and Paul knew that Devi would be pleased, and grateful, as he was, not only to the Lord, but also to the kind and thoughtful friends who had made it possible.

What a happy day when Paul received the telegram announcing Devi's flight! She would be there in time for Christmas! Happier still when, accompanied by two or three dozen friends, he went to the airport to meet her, bursting with suppressed excitement, wondering how she would look and how big Johnny would be. At fourteen months would he walk, and even talk . . . perhaps say "Dadda"?

The connecting flight from Honolulu arrived, the last leg on that long trip from Calcutta. As the passengers walked from the plane, many of them tanned and wearing Hawaiian leis, Paul's excitement grew wilder, then turned to apprehension, and finally into bewildered disappointment. No sign of Devi! Ed Murphy had an airline attendant check the passenger list. Devi's name wasn't on it. Had she had reservations? Yes, that was confirmed; but she hadn't been on the plane.

Listening to Ed relate what he'd learned, Paul found himself in the grip of a dark and horrible fear. "She'll be on tomorrow's flight, brother; she missed her connection," friends tried to assure him, but some deep inner voice told Paul it was a false hope. As Ed drove him home, he began to tremble, then broke into sobs.

"Look, brother," said Ed with concern, startled to see Paul in such a state, "I'll stay with you in your apartment tonight. Okay?"

They prayed for a long time together; and when Ed finally had to get some sleep, Paul was still on his knees weeping. Only later would he learn that Devi's flight from Tokyo to Honolulu had gone down somewhere in the Pacific without a trace or a survivor. He knew only that he felt an overwhelming sense of loss.

As he wept and prayed he was confronted by two questions: Was he willing to carry on the goal of a Bible college for India, even if it had cost him his wife and son? And in spite of all, would he still trust his heavenly Father's wisdom and care?

On his knees Paul struggled until he could say yes. He would trust and obey. But the pain, deep and searing, was still there.

11

The Hindustan Bible Institute

The next night found Paul at the airport again meeting the same connecting flight from Honolulu, trying to tell himself that Devi would be on it even though a deeper voice told him she wouldn't. Only a handful of friends came with him, the few out of that large reception committee of the night before who were willing to sacrifice another evening for a vague hope. Strangely enough, neither Paul nor any of his friends had noticed the newspaper article reporting the disappearance without trace of Devi's flight from Tokyo to Honolulu.

Again Ed Murphy drove Paul home after waiting in vain, watching the passengers disembark from the plane. Still no sign of Devi. It was another night of prayer for Paul—another night of weeping and soul-searching. Would he accept his Father's will without complaint? Did he still believe God loved him? The only possible answer to either question was an affirmative one.

Devi's last hours in India had been full of excitement and the sorrow of farewell. Sensing that disaster would result from this trip, her mother had cried for the last three days before her departure. Dr. Raju had accompanied his daughter on the train to the airport at Calcutta. Watching her plane lift from the ground, he had suddenly been seized with the horrible fear that he had done the wrong thing to put her on it, and he had fainted for the first time in his life. As India receded into the distance Devi had wondered whether she would ever see her land and her parents again.

Early the third evening, as Paul sat alone in his small apartment waiting for Ed to pick him up to go to the airport again, the phone rang. It was the airline—they had located Devi! They had no explanation for the delay, but she was on the passenger list of the flight coming in from Hawaii that evening. It seemed almost too good to be true! Paul called Ed Murphy and Bill Wood, and they notified many other friends.

There was a reception committee of about fifty waiting joyously to meet Devi when she came off the plane, carrying Johnny and two small handbags. The first moments of that tearful reunion were carried on in rapid Telugu, until Paul realized that no one else could understand. He began to interpret for Devi, who seemed too excited or too frightened to try her poor English.

"She doesn't speak English very well yet," said Paul to everyone crowding around. "That saved her life. In Tokyo she didn't understand the loudspeaker when it announced her flight to Honolulu, so she missed that one and had to spend the night in the airport. The next morning she learned that the flight she had missed had disappeared somewhere in the Pacific. I'm sorry for the many who were lost, but how I praise the Lord for sparing Devi and Johnny!"

Devi was pleased with the tiny apartment and so happy to be with Paul again. They decided to ask some friends to celebrate with them. Paul phoned Ed Murphy and Clyde Daly to invite them for dinner. "It's going to be chicken curry and rice, Indian style," he promised them. "You've never had anything like it!"

That certainly turned out to be true. Devi had never seen a refrigerator in her life, and had never heard of frozen food. She couldn't understand why the chicken Paul had bought was so cold and rockhard, unless that was the way American chickens were. Somehow she managed to cut it up; but it simply didn't cook and she didn't know why. Paul was too busy showing off Johnny to Ed and Clyde to do anything except remind Devi that their guests were waiting, and where was the food? So Devi dished up the curry, still wondering about those tough American chickens.

Ed and Clyde did their best to chew the raw meat, but husbands don't have to be polite. "What happened?" Paul exclaimed when he encountered his first piece of chicken-flavored leather. Devi was embarrassed enough to cry. Her first meal in America, and for guests, was a failure! Suddenly Paul understood the problem. "The chicken was *frozen,*" he explained, beginning to laugh at the look on Devi's face. "She's never seen anything like that. I forgot to tell her to thaw it—I've been so busy enjoying my son."

It hardly seemed to matter. Devi was there safely with Johnny. After a miracle like that, who could complain about anything else?

Devi enrolled in Biola for the February semester. It was hard to believe that she was only a year behind Paul. There was a nursery for Johnny: and in spite of her duties as housewife and mother, she managed to do very well in her studies, picking up English as she went along.

Paul was talking more and more about his primary purpose, and friends and even faculty members at Biola were beginning to take it more seriously. Dr. William Orr, at that time vice-president of Biola, and Dr. Feinberg, one of the professors, began to encourage Paul to organize a nonprofit corporation so that funds could begin to accumulate in preparation for the day when he would graduate and go back to India to start the school. Other staunch supporters of this idea were Dr. Jesse W. Baker, pastor of Calvary Baptist Church of Burbank, and William R. Litzenberg, an attorney, who volunteered to do the legal work.

It seemed rather ludicrous when a small, earnest group with nothing tangible, but lots of faith, met that Saturday afternoon, November 25, 1950, in Mr. Litzenberg's office on South Broadway for the organizational meeting of the board of directors of the Hindustan Bible Institute. The name had been suggested by Dr. Feinberg. "You can't call it the Indian Bible Institute," he had said, "because some people would think it was for American Indians. The Moslems call their country Pakistan, so a good word for India is Hindustan. Call it the Hindustan Bible Institute."

That first meeting didn't accomplish a great deal, but it was a start.

The statement of doctrine was discussed and it was decided to adopt Biola's rather than to write a new one. The board voted to get a post-office box and to open a bank account, although there was nothing to put into it. Paul had been receiving funds from church offerings and gifts from friends. From now on all funds would have to be turned over to the board. Nothing could be kept for himself. An initial monthly allowance for salary and expenses of $200 was voted for Paul, who was designated the "director" of the school that didn't yet exist. An executive committee was formed, and even an advisory council was discussed, to be composed of leading evangelicals such as pastors and evangelists. Paul was to design a letterhead, and Ed Murphy would write a pamphlet explaining the "Origin and Purpose" of the Hindustan Bible Institute. It was an optimistic group, talking and praying as though they really expected something to come of this school idea that Paul's friends in India still considered to be a wild scheme.

The first slogan the new board adopted was, "Send missionaries and train missionaries." The idea was that while there still seemed to be time they ought to send as many missionaries from the West into India as they could. The doors hadn't been officially closed, but their closing was anticipated shortly. Trained American Christians who were already established in their faith and had graduated from seminaries would be of great value getting the new school started.

In April 1951 the embryo organization received its first application from a couple who wanted to serve as missionaries in India. David Jones and his wife, Marion, were both graduates of Wheaton College, and David would complete his studies at Pasadena's Fuller Theological Seminary in May. They expected to spend the summer and fall raising support, and to leave for India the following January. Meeting with them, the board was very well impressed with their dedication to the Lord and their call to India. After prayer and much discussion they were accepted. David would be the first principal of the new school when it opened. The Jones family applied immediately for visas, and everyone waited breathlessly. They were to wait a very long time.

On their speaking tour in the summer of 1951, Paul and Ed Murphy, who had become the first treasurer of the board, met with the second missionary applicant, Edgar Dreschel, who was just finishing seminary training in the East. He came to Los Angeles to be interviewed by the board and was also accepted to be a teacher in the school. Immediately he, too, began to make plans to go to India. Departure for India of David and Marion Jones and their baby daughter had now been postponed until April 1952. Although visas had not yet been granted, the board was still optimistic, and at its February 1952, meeting it voted to have a special send-off banquet for the Jones family on March 21.

The April departure date came and went and still no visas. Investigation seemed to indicate that the problem was the fact that the Hindustan Bible Institute existed only on paper and had no actual work in India. The board decided that Paul must return to India immediately to rent a building and open the school, even though he had not yet finished his own training at Biola. He would act as the principal until David Jones arrived.

The new organization had no funds for Paul's air fare to India, so he set out for New York by car with Devi and a girl friend of hers who would accompany her back to Los Angeles. Before they had gone many miles the Lord had provided Paul's entire fare through an offering at the First Baptist Church in Walsh, Colorado, where Paul and Ed had previously held a week of special meetings and about forty people had received Christ.

Landing first in London, Paul spent two days with a number of his converts who had moved there from Kharagpur. These people had been among his closest friends in India and he expected them to help him with the costs of starting the school, but they were very cool toward the idea and contributed nothing except the guarded implication that he had gotten a big head in America and was still as impractical as ever. Paul found this same attitude among his friends in Madras when he arrived there and enthusiastically announced that he had returned to open the Bible school he'd been talking and praying about for so long.

"After a few months of studying in the United States," people would say, "the boy already wants to be the president of a Bible college. What delusions of grandeur!" A few said it to Paul's face, but most whispered it behind his back.

Still determined to listen to God and not to men, in spite of these discouraging responses from Christian friends, Paul rented a small house in the suburbs and began advertising for students for the "opening semester" in October. Rental for the house was about $20 per month—half of the personal tithe Paul had pledged for the project. It was two-storied with a large living room, not-so-large kitchen, and dining room on the ground floor, and two more rooms upstairs. It would be crowded—he fervently hoped—but adequate. After all, he wasn't planning anything like Moody or Biola, just a small school. Maybe the word *Institute* was a little grand after all. Well, they already had the letterheads, so it was too late to change that.

A few weeks after Paul's arrival Edgar Dreschel entered the country under a six-month tourist visa. It had been the only way to get into India quickly, and he expected to be able to renew his stay as a tourist until he could eventually get a resident visa. He accompanied Paul on a trip south to Mysore, where Paul took movies of a Hindu festival. The pictures would be invaluable back in the United States: Christians there had such a vague idea about Indians and Hinduism. This would help them to understand the need for training new missionaries to carry the Gospel to the 600,000 villages without a single Christian in them. On their way back to Madras, Paul stopped at Bangalore, with its memories, to visit his old friend Silas Fox, who was holding meetings there. Silas was overjoyed to see Paul again—but not very enthusiastic about his idea of starting a Bible school. Typical of most Plymouth Brethren at that time, he felt that formal instruction hindered the work of the Holy Spirit and made studying the Bible too much like studying mathematics or any other secular subject. Nevertheless he mentioned to Paul that his eldest son, Donald, who had been teaching for years at a Brethren school for missionaries' children, had just resigned his position.

"You ought to get in touch with him," said Silas. "He's praying for guidance from the Lord as to what he should do next."

"I'll send him a letter as soon as I get back to Madras," Paul promised.

Miracle of miracles, by the time the school was ready to open, five full-time students had been accepted. They would sleep in the dining room at night, study and eat in it during the day. As thrilled as if there were 500, Paul invited Christians in Madras to the "Inauguration Ceremony." More than 200 came and sat outdoors in the small yard on rented chairs. The head of public education for the entire state of Madras, a devoted and born-again Christian, was the master of ceremonies. One of the five students played his violin, another played a borrowed organ. The main speaker was the president of an evangelical seminary several hundred miles away that Paul had learned of only after going to America. He explained the need for training Indians to evangelize their own country. Paul also spoke on this theme, explaining that the Hindustan Bible Institute (that name sounded too grand for a small house with five students) would not—unlike a regular seminary—be so much interested in producing pastors to take over established churches, but would develop evangelists to pioneer in areas where Christ was not known and to establish new congregations. This was the passion that had driven him since the day he had wept beside the tiny fresh grave of his firstborn son. By God's grace it would yet be fulfilled!

Together with his wife, Donald Fox arrived in December to take the leadership of the school. Paul stayed on until the middle of January, teaching classes and helping with the organization and administration. By now there was a night school going, with twenty-eight students, being taught by a missionary from a nearby Brethren Assembly.

Sometimes Paul would pace the floor of the garage where he was living, his heart bursting with praise to God for what He had done.

At other times, walking around the small rented property or standing in front of the five students teaching a class, he would be overwhelmed with the excitement and wonder of the fact that the school had actually begun. It wasn't much, and they didn't know where the money was coming from to support it—the students couldn't pay any tuition—but it was something, a start, and he was glad!

With the "Institute" thus brought to a trembling and unpretentious birth, Paul flew back to Los Angeles in the middle of January 1953 to rejoin his family and to resume his own training at Biola.

12

Faith . . . or Vain Hope?

"Now that we actually have the school going in India . . . I'm much more optimistic about getting missionaries in!"

With these words of good cheer Paul concluded his enthusiastic report at the January 31 board meeting upon his return from India. There was much praise and thanksgiving to the Lord for his goodness. Rejoicing, too, over the application received from a third couple, Mr. and Mrs. Bill Head, who wanted to go as missionaries to India, hoped to teach trades at the Hindustan Bible Institute.

"Get as many missionaries in as we can before the doors close!" With determination and considerable optimism this ambition was echoed and reechoed often during the evening, both in conversation and formal discussion.

It was, therefore, a severe blow when word came from Delhi a few months later that the Jones family would not be granted a visa. That was final. No appeal possible. This news was followed by word from Dreschel that he had been refused a renewal of his tourist visa and must leave India immediately. Sending him his return fare dangerously depleted the small bank balance, leaving the school in a precarious position with almost no operating funds. The board went on record against allowing any other missionaries to go to India on tourist visas.

Hope was kept alive, however, that the Heads would receive favorable consideration because Bill had applied to teach practical courses such as carpentry, electronics, and printing. Surely the Indian government would be in favor of *that*—and by learning a trade the graduates would be able to support themselves with jobs on the side while preaching the Gospel all over India. It seemed like a sound idea—which made it all the more inexplicable when the Heads, too, were denied entrance to India.

This created a major crisis for the young organization.

"It's now quite obvious that we can't send missionaries to India," David Jones began his persuasive argument to the board at its June 1953 meeting. "That being the case, I think this board should be dissolved. The whole thing ought to be carried on in India by Indians. If we can't send missionaries, then we shouldn't be involved at all!"

A long and heated discussion followed, heavily weighted in favor of David's proposal by the dramatically timed entrance into the room of Edgar Dreschel, whose ship had just docked in San Francisco. He had come immediately to Los Angeles to give the board his pessimistic report. Paul was crying to the Lord in his heart, knowing the abject poverty of India and the need for help from Christians in America. To his great relief, the board unanimously reaffirmed that the organization had been founded to help raise money for the support of a Bible school in India; and even though workers apparently could not be sent from this country, the school was desperately needed and should be supported. God had given a clear vision to Paul, and the members of the board, having also accepted this challenge from the Lord, would continue to fulfill their part.

At the following meeting the resignations of David Jones—chosen to be the Institute's first principal—and his wife were accepted with profound regret. David and Marion felt very strongly the call to a foreign field, and since India would not allow them to enter, they had decided to go to Honduras under another mission.

One small hope remained for getting missionaries into India. There were now several applicants who proposed to attend the University of Madras under student visas for advanced degrees and to teach at the Hindustan Bible Institute at the same time. Ed Murphy and his wife, Loretta, were among those hoping to enter India in this way

. . . but again the hopes were in vain. The struggling organization had no choice but to drop the "send missionaries" from its slogan, and to concentrate all attention and use its limited resources to "train missionaries" for India. Certainly Paul's original estimate of the effects of Independence had been proved correct, and the necessity to train Indians to evangelize their own country could not have been more vividly demonstrated. The school now had eight students registered for the new term. It was encouraging, if not spectacular, progress. Donald Fox reported that he was looking for a larger house to rent.

The following months passed quickly for Paul and Devi in an almost unbelievable whirl of studies, preaching tours from coast to coast, the establishment of many, many lasting friendships, three graduations—one each for Devi and Paul from Biola with bachelor's degrees, plus a master's degree for Paul from a Baptist seminary. Looking back upon less than five years in the United States, it seemed impossible to Devi that with everything else that had happened she had also further confounded the doctors by giving birth to three more healthy babies. The Gupta family had begun to feel as though they had always lived in this country that had seemed so frightening and strange at first. This was now their land and these were their people. The bonds of love with many friends had grown deep and strong.

So the excitement of returning to India was mingled with the sorrow of bidding farewell to many loved ones when Paul and Devi, with their four children, went to the Hollywood-Burbank airport to board a charter for London and Bombay one hot August day in 1955. Johnny was nearly seven years old, Ruth was about three, Paul (nicknamed Bobby) was just two, and Samuel was only six weeks old. There were tears in the eyes of many friends who came to send them off with gifts and earnest promises to pray for them and the growing school. As their plane lifted from the ground, Paul and Devi tried to explain to the excited children, who had known no home except Los Angeles, that "home" was really India, because that was where God had something very special for them all to do.

Dr. Raju, as excited and proud as any grandfather could be, met them in Bombay and accompanied them on the train to Narsapur. Walking once again through the old familiar house and out into the garden, showing her children where she had been raised, Devi was confronted with a kaleidoscope of memories: the joys of her childhood here; the sickroom with its memories of her surrender to the Lord's will to marry Paul; the condemnation and disapproval of friends and relatives and the predictions of disaster by so many when she had married him; the death of their firstborn and the fresh surrender to God's call to establish a school; the reproach this vision had brought, with the accusations of impracticality and insinuations of selfish ambitions. But all of that was in the past. She had been only nineteen when she left India. Now she was a woman, returning with four children of her own. The school had been established and was growing. Surely the difficult days of travel and study and conflict were gone forever. The future could only be good and full of joy.

While Devi remained with her parents, allowing them to enjoy their grandchildren a little longer, Paul hurried on to Madras to search for a suitable house near the school, arriving just in time for the first "graduation"—for one student. Of the five who had enrolled that first year, one had been expelled and another had dropped out. The other two would graduate the following year. Donald Fox called it "prize day," because not only was honor given to the one graduating, but there was a prize for each student who had attained high enough grades. It was a very emotional experience for Paul. Only one graduate—a very small thing—and still only a handful of students, but the Lord had begun to fulfill his promise. Looking out over the audience of about 500 in the Methodist church, participating in the "ceremony," feeling overwhelmed by God's goodness, Paul had to keep reminding himself that he wasn't dreaming . . . it *was* happening.

Paul found a house at last and the family was able to move to Madras. Devi's training at Biola was not to be in vain. She was able to teach several classes after Manoma arrived. Raised by Amy Charmichael since she had been orphaned at ten months of age, Manoma, who was now in her forties and a devoted Christian with a shining face and loving disposition, became like a grandmother to the children, taking the place of Devi's mother, who was soon to die unexpectedly.

The first crisis for the growing school came a few weeks after the Guptas had settled in their house on Balfour Road about two miles away. Paul was teaching some courses, but happened to be at home when Donald arrived at the door looking perturbed, his red hair glistening with raindrops. Short and muscular, he was a man of discipline and action, and there was a problem that needed immediate attention: the first student rebellion. Little did Paul realize that there would be more and bigger ones.

"You've got to come over to the school right away and let them know who's the *principal!*" he said, never a man to mince words. "Since you've returned from the States, I've had no end of discipline problems. The students won't do anything I say; they want to check it out with you first."

Paul wasted no time in calling the students together to tell them in plain terms that Donald Fox was the principal and that *everyone,* including Paul Gupta, took orders from him. "You're here to study the Word of God, to learn to follow Jesus Christ and to carry his Gospel to India," he reminded them sternly. "Whoever doesn't want to obey the Lord's servants doesn't want to obey him. Either follow the rules or leave the school!" It was Paul's first "ultimatum" speech, but he would make many more and become known as a man who "lays down the law." In the coming months and years he would discover that even though the students had come because of their devotion to Christ and their desire to preach in his name, Satan would never stop trying to stir up rebellion and discontent, and it must be dealt with firmly.

Donald Fox was also a strict disciplinarian, and a good administrator. He had already established many basic principles that would stand the test of time. Like Paul, he was determined that the school would not be merely academic, but intensely practical: an institute for developing missionaries to evangelize India and to establish new churches where Christ was not known. Each afternoon, after a full morning of classes, the students went out to preach in the streets, to distribute tracts, to sell Gospels, and to talk with Hindus wherever they could. For most of them this was a new experience, and how thrilled they were to stand together singing and playing instruments, watching the crowd gather quickly in the street around them, and then to preach Christ boldly to the listening Hindus and Moslems and to see the intense interest on many faces—and what rejoicing over those who came forward to kneel, weeping tears of repentance and receiving Christ! Few students could ever be the same again after such an experience. Although the school was still small, for Paul this was a dream come true.

One day who should appear at the door of their home on Balfour Road but Paul's brother—seventeen years since they'd seen each other! After all of the questions and catching up—both parents, and of course Jaigee, and many aunts and uncles were now dead—his brother explained why he had come. "Father said I should tell you the business is yours . . . if you'll become a Hindu again. Those were almost his last words, but he'd said it often when he would talk about you."

It broke Paul's heart to know that his father had died like that. Tears pouring from his eyes, he shook his head. "You become a Christian!" he pleaded. "You can keep everything. I don't need it— I have the Lord. There is forgiveness of sins, it's really true!"

But Paul's attempt to persuade his brother to receive Christ seemed to fall on deaf ears. He had come to make the offer, honoring their father's dying request. Nothing more. He excused himself and left— the business was prospering and he had to hurry back to it. With tear-dimmed eyes and aching heart Paul followed the receding figure as long as he could still see him walking down Balfour Road toward Kelly's Corner trying to hail a passing cab.

Before Paul's return, the school had moved into a new building: a two-storied brick-and-plaster structure set back behind a business establishment on a side road about two blocks from Jehovah Shamah.

The Foxes lived upstairs, and the enlarged student body of fourteen full-time students had their dormitory downstairs next to the kitchen and the dining room that doubled for a classroom. But the need for a still larger facility was acute. There were now more applicants than they could accommodate, and the reports being received from graduates left no doubt that the school was worth expanding.

Paul and Donald looked at a larger house, but the price was $20,-000, which ended the matter. They had no money. In fact the financial situation had reached a crisis. The board wrote to Paul early in 1956 to inform him that since his departure the monthly income had dropped drastically. Unless it improved quickly the school would die on the vine without producing the fruit that everyone had prayed and worked so hard for. It hardly seemed a likely time to be thinking of expanding or purchasing a piece of property, but the need was there, and Paul knew that the Lord would provide.

"As you know, I'm not in favor of the school's becoming very large," Donald reminded Paul one day. "I want to see quality rather than mere quantity. But I hear that the Strict Baptist Mission wants to sell its property over on Madavakkam Tank Road."

"I know the place well," replied Paul thoughtfully. "It must be very expensive. A lot of land and a large dormitory . . . with a solid bungalow. . . ." He was staring out a window, trying to quell the growing excitement he suddenly felt. It couldn't be. There was no use in dreaming an impossible dream. His critics were right—he *was* impractical and visionary. He turned back to face Donald and reality. "I'll be wasting my time, but anyway I'll go over there and see how much they want for it."

The property was located on the edge of one of the better suburbs, near Kelly's Corner, just over the narrow bridge spanning a shallow muddy tributary where someone was always beating wet clothes on a rock, or grazing undernourished goats and water buffaloes, or defecating. Leaving Madavakkam Tank Road with its honking taxis, lumbering bullock carts, bicycle rickshas, wandering cows and hurrying pedestrians, Paul followed a narrow dirt road for a hundred yards along the river bank before it turned abruptly to the right in front of a three-storied dormitory, overgrown with vines, that looked abandoned. Directly in front of him, through the towering tamarind trees, he could see the sprawling missionary bungalow with the stone church fifty feet to the right just beyond the tall dormitory. This had once been a thriving mission compound, but it now looked deserted. Another reminder of the changes that had followed Independence, and a portent of things yet to come.

Nearly three acres! Room for expansion! In his mind he could see other buildings springing up in the future as the Lord provided the funds. *Could it be true? It could be . . . and it would be!* He had that deep conviction now. It wasn't his impractical optimism, but God's will.

Minutes later, however, sitting on the porch listening to Mr. Kurt, the missionary in charge, Paul wasn't so sure anymore. *Strange how faith and vain hope are so similar—and so hard to distinguish at times.*

"We've been offered 50,000 rupees. Cash." Mr. Kurt had said that twice.

A lot of money! What was he doing here? He nodded absently and let his eyes wander over the property again. *The dormitory. The extra land. What God could do with this, if only. . . .*

"I hope you're interested. It would be ideal for you. We like what we've seen of your school . . . and I'll be perfectly candid, we'd prefer selling to someone like you. Our doctrinal views are so similar. I don't want to see this property in the hands of people who don't even believe in the inspiration of Scripture."

Paul knew he had to say something, but it was painfully embarrassing. Where was that confidence he had felt a few minutes ago? "I wish we could buy it, but our organization is so new, and so small . . . we really don't have any money."

Mr. Kurt was observing Paul closely, a half smile playing across his lips. "Paul, you've told me so many stories of how the Lord has always supplied your needs. . . ." He left the sentence unfinished, hanging in the hot, humid air.

Paul shifted uncomfortably. "You're right, brother. I really felt as I walked onto this property just now that this is what the Lord had in mind for us. If it is . . . I know he'll provide, no matter how impossible it seems. Let me contact our board, and pray about it. I'll be in touch with you."

"Don't take too long. We really have to do something soon."

As he left the bungalow and walked back across the broad property out to the main road, Paul was already praying, asking the Lord to deliver him from his own ambitions. "We want only your will, Lord. Make it plain." He knew that he must surrender even the desire that he felt within him for this property. But that didn't prevent him from looking it over with a careful eye. The brush would have to be cleared, and there was some low land to fill—but the bungalow was large and sound, and the dormitory, with some repairs and perhaps expansion, would accommodate about thirty students, twice the number now crowded into the small house they were renting. No stranger to property values, Paul was sure it was worth more than 50,000 rupees. Where would the money come from?

With the board's encouragement, but with no promise from them of funds, Paul—after much prayer—offered 64,000 rupees: 30,000 to be paid by December 31, 1956, and the remainder over the next five years. The Strict Baptist Mission accepted the offer and the board approved the purchase in principle but could not promise the money. Paul had felt that any offer of less money down or at a later date would not have been accepted. Now it was up to the Lord.

Paul had often told friends, "Donald Fox saves more money than he spends; he's *very* conservative." This unbelievable frugality had accumulated 15,000 rupees from the monthly budget allowance sent by the American board over the four years the school had been in existence. That was half of the down payment. Although the other 15,000 rupees wasn't in sight, Mr. Kurt decided to let the Institute occupy the property immediately. He moved out of his side of the bungalow, allowing the Fox family to move in. The other half was still occupied by a Mr. Appleby and his family. They would remain until the balance due December 31 had been paid.

What an exciting day in October 1956 when the faculty and students helped to move the furniture—a few benches, bookshelves, tables, and cots—on rented bullock carts through the midday traffic of shouting vendors, meandering cows, and careening taxis. When that was done, everyone gathered in the Foxes' new quarters to praise the Lord for his faithfulness and grace. One after another, fervent prayers were offered dedicating the property to God for the evangelization of India.

There was much work to be done. The dormitory hadn't been used for years. Vines and brush had grown in through doors and windows; rats and snakes had made it their den. It seemed there would be no end of cleaning debris, hoeing weeds, and clearing brush. Everyone pitched in with great joy. Songs of praise to the Lord mingled with the sound of rakes, hoes, axes, and falling trees. There were many deadly cobras living on the property, and these began to be discovered as the jungle was gradually cleared. One day Devi and Paul were talking together under a tall tamarind tree between the bungalow and dormitory, when a twelve-foot cobra dropped out of the branches and landed beside them. Grabbing a long piece of bamboo, Paul hit it on the head, killing it. Students ran up and cut off the frightful head, with its wide hood and bared fangs. On another occasion Devi was working at the desk in the bungalow study, when an eight-foot cobra crawled out from behind a bookcase and began slithering toward her. Hearing her screams, several students arrived almost immediately to kill the deadly snake. Their holes were everywhere. "A regular cobra zoo," was the way some of the students described the property in those days. About twenty cobras were killed and the rest moved out, apparently convinced that the bothersome humans had come to stay.

Of course, if the balance of the down payment were not made on time—and that was beginning to look more probable every day—the cobras would be able to come back. The Strict Baptist Mission Board was having second thoughts about having allowed the Institute to occupy the property. Obviously that decision had been premature. December was half gone and still there was no sign of money: just the hopeful—but unanswered—prayers of faculty and students. With the deadline of December 31 only two weeks away, Mr. Appleby, who was still living with his family in half of the bungalow, received instructions not to vacate the property under any circumstances until the full down payment had been received. He was advised not to trust Indians, particularly Paul Gupta, who was apparently a promoter with no real financial backing.

The precedent had already been firmly established to devote most of each Christmas vacation to a "Gospel tour" participated in by the entire school. Arrangements had been made for the 1956 crusade in Nellore, about 120 miles north of Madras near the Bay of Bengal. Should they go in spite of the uncertainty?

"The purpose of the school is to train new missionaries to spread the good news about Christ," announced Paul. "We'll go . . . and leave the financial burden with the Lord. It's beyond our power anyway."

Preaching daily in the streets, selling Gospels, conducting Bible classes, and holding a Gospel meeting in a church each night did not prevent the students and faculty from spending many hours together in fervent prayer asking the Lord to provide the 15,000 rupees on time. Christmas day was spent entirely in prayer and fasting, with the nervous knowledge that less than a week remained for this miracle to happen . . . if it was going to.

The following morning the students left on various trains to spend a few days at home before the resumption of school early in January. Paul and Devi returned to Madras, arriving late that night, determined to continue in prayer until the answer came. It was a time of great heart-searching for Paul. Had they done the right thing in contracting to buy this property without the money in hand? He had been sure of it at the time, but the Lord had not honored this step of faith with the necessary funds. Nor did it seem likely that the money would arrive in the next four days. What would they do then? Paul tried not to think of that. Better to pray than to worry. He had learned that long ago.

"If you expect to support the school with money from the United

States," Donald Fox had cautioned Paul more than once, "you're building on a foundation of sand."

"I don't care where the Lord brings the money from," Paul had replied. "India, or the States, or anywhere, it's all the same to me."

But maybe Donald was right. The moment of truth had come.

13

The New Missionaries

"Fifteen hundred rupees cabled to your bank. Stop. Okay to issue check for balance of down payment. Stop. William Orr, Chairman."

Standing on the front porch where he had received it, with Devi looking over his shoulder, Paul held the cable in trembling fingers and read it again. "Praise God!" they both said quietly, smiling at each other now, eyes glistening with tears. It was December 27, 1956.

When the students returned early in January, everyone gathered for a special time of praise and thanksgiving. Once again the property was dedicated to the Lord for spreading the Gospel throughout India. The Appleby family began to pack their belongings. On March 1, 1957, Paul and Devi and their four children moved into one side of the bungalow. The milestone event was marred by sadness because the Foxes were now packing their things and moving out of the other side. Their son had been born just after they had joined the school, and unless they returned to spend a year in Canada he would lose his Canadian citizenship. They had not been there themselves for a number of years. Their departure was a great loss to the school, but hopefully they would return.

There were twenty-eight students for the new school year that began in July: twenty men and eight women. To have women studying in the school at all was remarkable for India. There had never been any thought of admitting women—but a few months before one of the students had married. As a courtesy his wife had been allowed to enroll—and that had opened a Pandora's box. She had felt outnumbered by all the males in the classroom. A girl friend from her village wanted very much to enroll in the school too. Could she? *Please?* After discussion and prayer, the faculty approved her application. But where to house her? There was an ancient cattle shed with a solid frame and good roof. When the walls were plastered and a floor added, it became the first women's "dormitory." Now, just six months later, there were eight girls living in it. Remodeling had also begun on the men's dormitory to increase its capacity. But what about classrooms? Classes were being held in part of the dormitory—but that space was needed for sleeping quarters. With hundreds of thousands of villages in India still without a witness for Christ, how could anyone think of not expanding the school? Although there were no funds, *something* had to be done.

The budget to feed the students, pay minimal salaries to staff, and maintain the school, including monthly payment on the property, was now nearly $1,000 per month. This was being received from the American board, but there was nothing left over for construction of new classrooms. In fact, the board had written to tell Paul that income was lagging badly. The school was still largely unknown among Christians in the United States. Without publicizing it, which cost money, or without a miracle—or perhaps both—the board didn't know how much longer it could keep up the present level of support.

This problem weighed heavily upon Paul. The Lord had given them extra land. They must find a way to use it, money or no money.

"I think we should put up a cheap frame building with a thatched roof," Paul suggested at a faculty meeting. "It wouldn't cost much—and we could divide it into several classrooms if the teachers don't talk too loudly."

No one had a better suggestion, so he asked one of the students with some artistic ability to draw the plans to scale. The shed would be erected on a piece of ground that had been cleared of brush and trees in front of the bungalow. With the completed sketch, Paul drove to the city hall of Madras, where he presented it to the building department. Not at all in favor of giving a building permit for a thatched shed, they turned him down. On the way over from the school Paul's car had been slammed from the rear: and now this new blow added to the financial problems, the loss of Donald Fox, and the feeling of frustration at the smallness of the school in comparison to India's exploding population . . . it was too much. Was the Lord just testing him, or had he been abandoned? Feeling despondent, like a modern Job, Paul was inwardly complaining to the Lord as, with downcast eyes, he slowly descended the stairs to leave the building. A young clerk running up the steps two at a time almost bumped into him.

"Brother Gupta!" he exclaimed. "You look discouraged. Did you have some trouble?"

"Lots of it!" replied Paul in a defeated voice. "I want to build some extra classrooms, but they won't let me."

"Come back up with me," his friend suggested. "I know the head of the mechanical engineering department. He's a Christian—at least a nominal one. Let's tell him your problem."

Robert Moses recognized Paul immediately, having heard him preach in the church he attended. He was very friendly and eager to help. "You don't want to put up a thatched hut!" he exclaimed after glancing at the plans. "That isn't going to last . . . and you wouldn't be happy with it. You need something substantial."

"The problem is," said Paul, feeling embarrassed now, ". . . we don't really have the money to build even a thatched hut."

"Don't worry about that . . . yet," responded Mr. Moses, beginning to sound as though he felt personally responsible for expanding the school. "First of all, let's get some plans drawn for a reinforced concrete building. I'll get one of our architects to do them for practically nothing. I'll help you put it up at the lowest possible cost."

It will have to be lower than you can imagine, Paul was thinking. But he thanked Mr. Moses and drove back to the school, feeling as discouraged as he could ever remember in his life. After all of these years of prayer and work and struggle, the school had begun and had moved to a beautiful piece of property. He had thought that would mark a new era of success. Instead, the problems only got bigger and more impossible. Must the battle go on forever with no time for rest?

During the next few months the contributions coming into the Los Angeles office declined to the danger point, and the board increased its efforts to persuade Paul to return to the States for a speaking tour to present the school's needs to American Christians. He resisted that suggestion. There was too much work to be done here. Of course, there wasn't much one could do about building classrooms without money. The problem of money had been discussed in the past with Donald Fox: whether to tell Christians about the school's needs or to expect the Lord to tell them. Donald had been against "fund raising." Paul had agreed that there were many abuses in this area, but he still felt it was Scriptural to let God's people know of the needs. However, he didn't want to be the one to tell them if it meant leaving the school and his family to make an exhausting tour across the United States speaking every night in different churches.

Some of the tall tamarind trees with spreading branches that were gradually being cut down to clear the property were as much as nine feet around. Doors and planks were fashioned out of them. Sale of the extra lumber brought several thousand rupees: and with that money construction was begun on the new classroom building as soon as the plans were completed. It didn't take long for those meager funds to be exhausted. The cement supplier was willing to extend credit for two or three weeks—but the brick masons had to be paid each Saturday, and the supplier of sand demanded payment for each load. Without cash in hand the construction came to a complete halt. The faculty and students gathered with Paul for a prayer meeting on the half-completed foundation. They soon learned that this building was to be erected literally by prayer. Money came in, construction resumed, funds were exhausted, construction stopped. The cycle became familiar. Again and again the students and faculty members joined Paul to sit or kneel first upon the foundation and then upon the rising walls, where they cried to their heavenly Father for more funds to continue the work. It was an odd sight for Hindu laborers or visitors to behold. But they were able to see that the Christian God answered these prayers. Slowly but steadily the money came in: some from India, most of it from the United States.

When it came time to frame the windows and doors as the walls extended upward, Paul noticed twenty heavy posts made of indestructible and costly Burma teak supporting the bungalow roof. Replaced by six inexpensive concrete pillars, the teak posts became the framing material for doors and windows, eliminating a major cost. A man in Madras donated 1,000 rupees just in time to buy rafters to support the roof, and Dr. Hugh Murchison sent $1,000 to purchase the corrugated asbestos sheets to lay on the rafters. At long last the building was done—and just in time! There were now forty students, and about sixty in the night school.

True to his word, Robert Moses had come to check the construction every afternoon on his way home from work. His help, which he donated without cost, was invaluable: but he also benefitted in a way he hadn't expected. The faith of the students and faculty, and the conversations Paul had with him about Christ, soon convinced Mr. Moses that in spite of his years as an active church member, he was lacking the personal relationship with the Savior that those at this school obviously enjoyed. Throwing away his cigarette just outside the gate, although no one had condemned him for smoking, he felt almost afraid to come onto the property to face these people whose godly lives convicted him of his own lack of submission to Christ. Yet there he was every evening, taking measurements, giving directions to the workers for the next day, and listening with amazement to the spontaneous and joyful witness Paul and others at the school bore to the abundant life in Christ. Opening his own heart, he experienced the new birth. Not long afterward, an evangelist held special meetings in his church, and Robert Moses went forward to make a public confession that he had received Christ as his personal Lord and Savior. That was the beginning of a new life.

About 300 applicants had already been turned away for lack of housing since the school had begun. A nominal tuition was now being charged—not so nominal for poverty-stricken India, where a laborer earned $15 a month—but still the applications poured in. The new classroom building was already inadequate. Happily, Mr. Moses, now a radiant Christian and dedicated member of the newly formed Indian board of directors, informed Paul that the foundation had been designed to support two more floors. The roof was taken off, and construction of a second floor begun, which would provide space not only for more classrooms but also for a much needed library. This was one of the requirements for affiliation with Serampore University, which would give the graduates accredited degrees for their work.

By the fall of 1959 there were fifty full-time students living at the school, crowded into outgrown facilities, and ninety taking night classes. Once again the roof was raised and a third floor was put on top to be used for supervised study in the evenings as well as for classes during the day. It was no longer possible to house the increased number of women students in the converted cattle shed, so construction of a proper women's hostel was begun in 1960, along with a dining room and kitchen. Quarters for married students were begun in 1962. Paul was kept busy day and night supervising construction, paying laborers, dealing with materials suppliers. Often he would be called out of a class he was teaching to handle a crisis at the construction site of a new building or a floor being added. Still the school was not large enough and funds were not adequate, either for the needed expansion or for the increased monthly budget that rose to $2,000, then to $3,000, then $4,000 . . . $5,000. It was prayer alone that brought in the funds and solved the many problems. Again—and again and again—Paul returned to the United States to inform churches and Christian friends of the progress the school was making and the need to expand even more. Graduates were seeing gratifying and God-honoring results in many parts of India, but many more graduates were needed. The harvest was great and the laborers still far too few.

The long hours and strenuous trips with changes in food and climate were wearing on Paul's health, but he couldn't stop. His frequent and sometimes lengthy absences brought a special kind of problem to

Devi, who remained at home with the growing children, doing correspondence for the school and also teaching. When Paul was away, false rumors would inevitably begin to circulate: that Devi was running after another man, or that Paul had abandoned her and would not return from his latest trip. These reproaches she bore silently, trusting the Lord to let the truth be known to those who wanted to know it. There are always some who love to listen to gossip, and it is useless to defend oneself to them. Paul's dedication to the school and extended trips to the United States, almost yearly now, were causing other problems within his own family. As the children grew older, they began to resent the long hours he worked while at home and the prolonged absences. They sometimes accused their father of caring for the school but not for them. That was difficult for Paul or Devi to explain to them.

Devi was able to make up for much of this with the girls (a second girl, Dolly, had been born after the fourth boy, Danny), but boys need a father. Paul was keenly aware of that. However, the Lord had given him a work to do, and—although it kept him too much from his family—if *he* didn't do it, who would?

That had been a costly lesson, at the very beginning, when they had used the coming birth of their first child to excuse them from obeying the Lord's call. The Lord had taken the child away. Now it seemed that their obedience to that call was bringing suffering to their children, and breeding resentment and sometimes rebellion. This was one more problem they would have to leave in the hands of the One who knows best, trusting him to work it out in his time and in his way. He had never failed them in anything, and they were confident that in this important matter he would be faithful as always.

The hard work was not without its rewards. By 1964 there were 100 students at the school. The greatest thrill was to have among them a number of converts of the many graduates who were now preaching the Gospel in thirteen Indian states. Paul was overwhelmed by God's grace. Excerpts from a letter he wrote at this time to Mrs. Granaas, a close friend in the United States, tell the story of those strenuous but joyous days.

How I am thrilled to see that some of our graduates who went out and are working in different fields are able to send some of their converts to our institute to study the Word! We are really very happy to say that their labors and ministry are bringing forth much fruit.

You will be much pleased to know that we have students in our school representing eight different languages of our country. How wonderful it is to see what God has done for us. May we have representatives for every language spoken in India. I am grateful to His people and to the Lord for all the things He has done for this school in a short time. It humbles me to think of the faithfulness of God. Please remember us while we train these young people for the Lord's cause.

I am taking Mr. Silas Fox to my native place to speak to my relatives and friends. He was well liked in the past so we are hoping that the Lord will bless our meetings there. I am very busy with the activities here and I need your prayers that the Lord may keep me and use me for the furtherance of the Gospel.

My wife . . . often suffers from pain. Johnny and Ruth were baptized last Sunday and we are very happy. Bobby also is saved and wants to be baptized. We covet your prayers for them that they may grow in the grace and knowledge of our Lord Jesus Christ.

14

The Lord Is Faithful

In the mid sixties the monsoons failed. In spite of all the rituals performed to the Hindu deities in thousands of temples by priests and worshipers pleading for rain, large sections of India were suffering from the worst drought in 100 years. In Madras, many staples, such as rice, were rationed. The faculty and students were forced to stand in long lines, sometimes until late at night, to get their meager share. Some Indian states, blessed by rain, actually had a surplus, but in spite of much talk at high levels about sharing with those in need, little food moved across state borders. Over Nehru's protests, India had been divided on the basis of language. Parliament had surrendered to the hate-inspired rioters who, all over India, had demanded that each language group have its own state. This ancient animosity remains so deeply rooted that all attempts of the central government in Delhi to adopt an official national language from among the fourteen major Indian tongues have failed. Madras itself had been the scene of bloody riots against the edict that Hindi would be the official language. This linguistic jealousy caused staunch Hindus, the advocates of nonviolence, to kill one another. School children in Europe were giving up their lunch money to feed India's starving millions—but the Telugu-speaking state of Andhra Pradesh refused to share its surplus with its Tamil-speaking neighbor state in which Madras is located.

Paul wrote to tell the American board that the students were half-starved, which made it difficult for them to study; and he asked for authorization to purchase their own land outside the city on which they could raise rice to tide them over in just such emergencies as they now faced. This request was approved, and one of the directors, through a family foundation, contributed $3,000, with which Paul was able to purchase ten acres of good paddy land. Devi took over this project, bought the rice, had the land plowed and fertilized, saw to the planting of the seed, weeding, and constant care that was required. She was kept busy going back and forth to the rice land and nursing along the crop, which turned out to be a good one and relieved the situation at least temporarily.

Such problems, while serious, were not allowed to interfere with the work and growth of the school. The year 1967 saw the completion of the new building needed to accommodate the expanding printing ministry, which had a most unlikely beginning. In the early fifties, while preaching in Walsh, Colorado, Paul had noticed an ancient press used by the First Baptist Church for printing its weekly bulletin. The pastor had remarked that it was eighty years old and that in the early mining days the town newspaper had been printed on it. "I could use a press like that in India for printing tracts!" Paul had exclaimed, half to himself, half aloud. "You can have this one," had been the pastor's immediate response, ". . . if you can get it over there." Preaching in the next town, Paul had mentioned this incident, and someone in the congregation who owned a truck had volunteered to take the press to Los Angeles harbor. Shipped to Madras, it had eventually cleared Indian customs and been delivered to the school, where it sat gathering dust until Paul returned and put it into use. Printing tracts for other Christian organizations, the school earned enough to buy another press, then another. Contributions came in for still more presses. Set up originally in part of the bungalow that had once been the Foxes' bedroom, the press had been moved eventually to its own building, and now that was enlarged to make room for this growing work. There were now five presses of various kinds and sizes, capable of printing 1.5 million tracts and several book editions of 10,000 each every month. From profits the press department was able to supply the school with the 2 million copies of tracts and booklets the students gave away annually at street meetings and from door to door. By the early seventies hardly a day went by without at least one letter arriving to tell of someone who had received Christ through the literature being printed in several of the major Indian languages.

By far the most mail, however, was being received in response to the school's own radio programs being beamed into India from three locations. Several rooms on the ground floor of the three-story concrete building that Paul had originally planned as a thatched hut had been converted into a first-class radio studio, fully equipped, sound-proofed, and air-conditioned, the air-conditioning a real necessity in that unbearably hot and humid climate. One of the school's graduates was sent to the Delhi offices of Back-to-the-Bible Broadcast for training to take charge of this important and fruitful work. The first broadcasts began in 1962 and have been increased in number and languages several times since then. All programs were recorded in the school's own studios. About 40,000 letters are received each year from listeners, many of them from those who have received Christ through listening to the broadcasts. One letter with forty signatures told of an entire village that had come to Christ and wanted a pastor to be sent to them.

In 1970 a new dormitory for men was begun. Eventually the ground floor was converted to badly needed administrative offices . . . and also included Calvary Memorial Chapel, which would seat about 300. This building, too, was literally built by prayer, one floor at a time. Sometimes the answers to prayer seemed to indicate that the Lord had a sense of humor—as, when funds were exhausted, stopping construction on the ground floor, two checks in identical amounts of $3,000 arrived the same week from new donors, one living in Australia and the other in New Mexico . . . and both with the same last name, *Brown!* With this $6,000 a concrete ceiling and roof were added to the walls, which became the floor of the second story. As with every other building, the funds came in steadily as the school prayed—but this time there was something new. When the fourth and final floor had been completed, the money continued to come in unsolicited. "I believe we ought to put up some shops and apartments on the commercial land we own that fronts on Madavakkam Tank Road," Paul wrote to the American board. When next in Los Angeles he discussed this in detail. "One of my burdens is to make the school as self-supporting as possible," he explained to the board, "and this would help. We could rent the shops, and above them we could build apartments to be rented also. Together they would provide a good monthly income."

With the board's approval the project was begun, and again after much prayer it was completed. A bank and post office and numerous retail shops quickly rented the space available, and the apartments above them were soon filled, bringing a net income of about $1,000 each month. Not a great deal in relation to the $8,000 current monthly budget for the school, but a step in the right direction.

Still the young men and women desiring to receive training as missionaries to their own country exceeded the space available. Completion of the fourth floor on the new men's dormitory left the school with a new problem: there was no more land for further expansion, yet the need was greater than ever. Since 1963 Paul had claimed for the Lord and the school the adjoining four-acre parcel fronting on the small river. Often students and faculty had gathered with him on that vacant property for a prayer meeting, asking the Lord to open the way for the school to have it, but the owner had steadfastly refused to sell it at any price. Still the prayers continued, prayers of faith, believing, as Paul often expressed it, that "the Lord is faithful." Then the miracle occurred, the nature of which was a complete surprise.

The government passed a new law limiting the amount of land an individual could hold. The owner of this adjoining parcel had far too much. Now he came to Paul, pleading with him to buy the land, and offering it at a bargain price. Although there were no funds, Paul felt it would be unthinkable to pass up this opportunity that the Lord had given them after so many years of believing prayer. Paul went to Los Angeles to present the opportunity to the Board. The purchase of the land was approved, with the minutes noting that the board didn't know where the money would come from and Paul would have to negotiate the price and terms on the basis of his faith in God to bring in the funds. That decision was honored by the Lord. Never in its history had the Institute received so much money in such a short period of time, much of it from unexpected sources. A woman Paul had met in Bend, Oregon, on that first summer's preaching tour with Clyde Daly died suddenly, and her estate of about $25,000 was given to the Institute. Other sums came in, large and small, and within a few months the entire purchase price of $90,000 had been paid, and the Institute owned it free and clear.

Returning from that trip to the United States, Paul visited Mr. Kidd in London. The former headmaster from Kharagpur, who had been about to commit suicide when Paul had been prompted by the Holy Spirit to come to his house, was still going on well for the Lord. "You can't imagine what I'm doing now," he told Paul with considerable excitement in his voice. "When I moved here they wouldn't honor my degrees earned in India. So instead of teaching mathematics and science to the English children, I'm teaching them the Bible—and being paid for doing it by the British government! If ten years ago you had tried to tell me this would happen, I couldn't have believed it. Isn't it wonderful the way the Lord works?" Paul could say a hearty "Amen!" to that and really mean it. Looking back over the years filled with God's blessings, he could testify that the greatest miracles were those involving the transformation of lives. There was nothing so satisfying as to see converts from the past, like the Kidds, still living for the Lord. His cousin, "Happy Paul," was still traveling about preaching the Gospel and had established several assemblies. The first woman student, allowed into the school with trepidation, had married another student, M. A. Thomas, and they were still carrying on a good work for the Lord in northern India. The very first graduate of the school was still preaching the Gospel and seeing lives changed by its power. The first married couple to be in the school were still serving the Lord faithfully. Hundreds of graduates were spreading the Gospel all over India, yet in spite of these great blessings, Paul could not help being troubled that he had not reached anyone in his immediate family for Christ.

Since his brother had come to see him ten years before to offer him his share of the family wealth if he would return to Hinduism, nothing had been heard from him. Then one day, there he was in the drive outside the bungalow, asking one of the students if this was where Vankateswami Gupta lived. Hearing his voice, Paul rushed out onto the porch, calling to him. After an emotional few moments of reunion, his brother began to unburden his heart—and what a tale of woe he had to tell!

"I have lost everything, Vankateswami!" he wailed. "Everything!"

"But that's not possible . . . how could you?"

"Our village did not prosper; there was a curse on it from the gods, so we moved. I became partners with a man I thought was my friend. All of my money was put into merchandise and sold to customers that he knew and I didn't. They wouldn't pay. He could collect from them, but I couldn't—yet he wouldn't do anything. Then one night when I visited him in his home, he and his sons tied me up and threatened to kill me unless I let them have the business." He was talking rapidly in a voice that begged for help. "My wife said I must leave. It wasn't safe to stay. I thought that you might be able to get the police to do something. . . ."

"If it had happened in Madras I could," said Paul sympathetically. "But that's 200 miles away and in another state. The Madras police have no jurisdiction there. Why didn't you go to the police in your own district?"

"It would do no good. They are afraid of him. Even if they arrested him, he would be released . . . and it would not be safe for me to stay there."

"Do you have no other money?"

"Nothing. All of my wife's gold and jewels I loaned to another friend. But now he says he can't pay me. I am left with *nothing!*"

"So you need a place to live far from your enemies?"

He nodded, a look of hope in his eyes.

"I have a place for you," said Paul. His voice broke and he had to look away. A wave of memories swept over him: the day he had given up his father's riches for the sake of Christ; the day his brother had offered those riches back if he would only become a Hindu again . . . and now those riches were no more. His brother had nothing— and he had everything. How true Christ's words: "Lay not up for yourselves treasures upon earth, where moth and rust doth corrupt, and where thieves break through and steal: But lay up . . . treasures in heaven . . ." (Matthew 6:19, 20).

Controlling his voice with difficulty, Paul said, "We have some paddy land outside the city, and the tenant we had working it for us has left. I am looking for someone . . . would you like the job? There is a small house there. . . ."

His brother looked relieved and grateful. "I would do a good job for you," he said eagerly. "My wife and I would be happy to live there. Where is it?"

The once hostile attitude of his remaining relatives began to soften after Paul's brother moved to the school's paddy land. Clearly this God of the Untouchables had been good to Vankateswami: he had traveled often to the United States and Europe and many countries; the school was on a large property with high buildings and 200 students; and he had been able to help his brother when he was in need by providing him with a house and a job . . . and yet when he had been put out of his home at the age of eighteen, penniless and under the curse of the gods, everyone had expected him to fail miserably. The God of the Christians had power—his relatives were convinced of that—but they were not yet willing to believe on Jesus alone. To them he was still one of the gods, a powerful god it seemed, but not the only God—and each of them had his own favorite deities. But as often as Paul and Devi saw his brother and his wife they spoke to them carefully about Christ, sharing the Gospel message that graduates of the Institute were preaching in towns and villages across India. It was hard to tell what the response was, other than gratitude for having been given shelter and employment.

"We are so busy that we always make excuses when we're invited to one of my cousins' homes," Paul said to Devi one day. "We should go to that wedding of my nephew in Proddutar next week. It would be a good chance to see many of my relatives again."

"I was thinking the same thing," replied Devi. "I would like to go. I've never seen the town where you grew up. Let's drive by it on our way."

Paul's pulse beat faster when he turned off the paved road onto the dirt lane—it still looked the same—then drove slowly through the Untouchables' village, beyond which lay his old hometown of Dugganapalli.

"There's the chapel where I was baptized the first time!" he exclaimed to Devi. "I walked past it that night when I was put out of my home. Around the next bend you'll see where I lived."

But coming around that familiar bend Paul received a shock. There was no village! Dugganapalli had vanished! Only the shell of the Rama temple remained. Even his own house was gone, every stick and stone removed—nothing left!

At the wedding they learned the story. A curse seemed to settle upon the village after Paul had left. No one thought it was judgment from his God for the way they had treated him. The priests said that the displeasure of their own gods had somehow been incurred. Business declined steadily for no reason. Nothing the residents of Dugganapalli did seemed to prosper. Every attempt was made to appease the gods, but the curse remained. Finally the priests seemed to agree upon the problem: the temple to Siva had been erected in the wrong location, and the gods were angry. The only hope was to move the whole village. People tore down their houses board by board, brick by brick, and moved them to a new location chosen by the priests, who transported all of the gods and reconstructed the temple there. But the curse remained. Gradually, one by one, families tore their houses apart and moved them again, to different communities this time. Dugganapalli was no more.

"What a lesson!" said Paul to Devi as they drove back to Madras after the wedding. "They thought I lost everything when I had to leave home. In fact, I *gained* everything. They are the ones who lost all!"

Devi nodded. "And what a tragedy it would have been if you had decided that your father's wealth was worth more than Christ! You would have nothing today!"

"It is a lesson I will never forget!" said Paul solemnly. "I wonder if it means anything to my brother and his wife."

That question was answered the next time he saw his brother. "There's a movie producer and his wife who became Christians through reading my testimony distributed by some of our students," Paul mentioned in the course of conversation, hoping to encourage his brother to do likewise. "They want to be baptized . . . to let the world know they've left their false gods. I'm going to baptize them in the ocean next week."

His brother sat quietly for some time, seeming to be deep in thought. "You have never asked me and my wife if we wanted to be baptized," he said at last.

"Do you?" asked Paul, hardly able to believe his ears.

"We are Christians now, too. Months ago we decided . . . but we didn't know how to tell you. Will you baptize us, too?"

Some of the students from the school came along to witness this happy occasion. It was not a beach for swimming, in spite of the broad sweep of clean sand and the sparkling water—the sharks saw to that. But it was a good place, and time, for praising God. There were tears in Paul's eyes when he waded ashore with his arm around his brother. "The Lord is faithful!" he said in a loud voice as though he wanted all of Madras to hear. "The Lord is faithful!" There were no better words for expressing the way he felt.

The long, thin leaves of the tall, stately asoka trees bordering the drive where it curves past a corner of the three-story classroom building hung limply in the still, oppressively hot morning air. Students were hurrying to their classes. The twenty-nine orphans, all under ten years old, who were living with the Guptas had just marched by in well-ordered column, holding hands two abreast on their way to school. "Good morning, father!" In unison with happy voices they had called out to Paul where he sat on the front porch reminiscing over the past with a tall and elderly friend. Bishop Joseph, in Madras for a conference of bishops, laughingly told Paul that he had never expected the school to amount to anything. "The Lord is faithful," replied Paul characteristically, and his old friend nodded his agreement. Indeed the Lord was faithful—no doubt about that. Those words were the story of Paul's life, the story of the Hindustan Bible Institute.

Paul shared his vision for the land they had just acquired next door: the large auditorium, a new men's dormitory and another one for women, a modern hospital, a grammar school. The plans were being prepared by an architect. It would all cost about $500,000—more than they had ever asked the Lord for, but Paul was confident the funds would be provided. The Lord was faithful. The hospital would be a ministry and at the same time it should support not only itself but the school too, fulfilling an ambition of many years.

But no matter how exciting the future seemed, the two old friends found themselves coming back again and again to the past, reminding one another of forgotten details from those bygone days when they had traveled together by bullock cart, from village to village, preaching in the streets. There was so much to remember. One subject, however, never came up: baptism. Each knew and respected the other's belief, and regretted the breach that had come between them because of this difference. In heaven there would be no arguments over such things. By unspoken mutual consent they had decided to experience, in the warmth of Christ's love, a little of heaven here on earth. And why not? It wasn't too early for that.

Imagine him a *Bishop* now, Paul thought, as his friend threw his head back and that familiar, warm laugh rolled out. How strange— and shameful—that he had once regarded this kind and godly man as an Untouchable. As an Untouchable without caste, beyond reach of the gods. An offering from such a lowly being would not be accepted by a Brahmin, for it would defile him. Yet because of sin all men were "untouchables." Krishna could only condemn them. It was for such that Christ had died. Hindus still call Him the God of the Untouchables. And He is.

Glossary

ahimsa A cardinal doctrine both of Hinduism and Buddhism that holds all life to be sacred and forbids violence against any living thing, yet fails to recognize that life is taken when the vegetarian boils water for his tea or chews a carrot.

avatar The incarnation of a god who has come to earth to lead his species upward toward oneness with Brahman. Some Hindus hold that animal species have their avatars also.

dharma Right behavior according to Hindu law, but it varies for every man, so each must discover his own dharma.

dhoti A long piece of cloth worn by Indian men, wrapped around like a skirt, sometimes tucked up in the middle to form baggy, short pants.

guru Literally a teacher, one who through the practice of one of the many paths to god-consciousness is able to lead others. Many Hindus believe that each person must have a guru or he cannot evolve upward to oneness with Brahman.

hare Rama, hare Krishna An exclamation of praise to Rama and Krishna, in Hindu mythology believed to be two of the reincarnations of Vishnu the Preserver, who is one of the three main gods, the others being Brahma the Creator, and Siva the Destroyer. Every 4.5 billion years Siva destroys everything, Brahma re-creates everything, and Vishnu appears again upon earth as a man to show men the way of life.

karma A law or force that repays every living creature in its next reincarnation for its deeds done in the present one.

mantra   One or more words constituting a prayer to a Hindu deity whose repetition is used to induce the mental state for meditation, or which is efficacious by mere repetition.

maya   The term applied to everything except Brahman under the teaching that all but the Absolute (Brahman) is illusion.

puja   A Hindu form of worship devoted to the gods, performed privately by the individual as well as publicly by a priest. There are many forms.

Vedanta   Another name for the Upanishads, which are the last of the Vedas. It can refer to the teachings of the Upanishads, the Upanishads themselves, or to that specific Hindu sect bearing this name and founded by Vivekananda to perpetuate the teachings of Ramakrishna. There are Vedanta temples in many major cities in the United States and around the world.

Vedas   The earliest of the Hindu sacred writings, composed of hymns, prayers, chants, liturgical formulas, and incantations—as opposed to the mythology narrated in the later writings such as the Bhagavad-Gita, Mahabharata, Ramayana.

yoga   A system of withdrawing from the illusion of the physical world to concentrate upon the Absolute in an effort to identify oneself with the Absolute and eventually achieve oneness with It.

yogi   A title given to one who practices yoga and has attained some proficiency in it.